How To Play & Win
THE COLLEGE GAME

A College Success Guide For New Students

Sharon Padilla-Alvarado

outskirtspress
DENVER, COLORADO

How To Play & Win The College Game
A College Success Guide For New Students
All Rights Reserved.
Copyright © 2015 Sharon Padilla-Alvarado
v4.0

Cover Photo © 2015 thinkstockphotos.com. All rights reserved - used with permission.

Outskirts Press, Inc.
http://www.outskirtspress.com

ISBN: 978-1-4787-5141-0

Outskirts Press and the "OP" logo are trademarks belonging to Outskirts Press, Inc.

PRINTED IN THE UNITED STATES OF AMERICA

Here's what the experts are saying about _How To Play & Win The College Game_

How To Play & Win The College Game **is a "game-changer" for new college students –** especially those who know little about the challenges they are about to face. **Author Padilla-Alvarado does a masterful job of speaking directly to students with practical advice** on knowing their faculty members, attending class, managing time and money, staying healthy and succeeding in college. Many of the lessons in this book are too often learned by students only as they are completing college. _How to Play & Win_ allows the new student to learn the ways of successfully navigating the college environment before the end of the first semester. **If you want to succeed in college read _How to Play & Win The College Game!_**

**Dr. Brice W. Harris**   _**Chancellor of the California Community Colleges**_

As a first-generation college graduate, I know first-hand the struggles facing college students pursuing a college degree. The information contained in this book is a tool for all students in pursuit of college success and completion, and in particular students coming from disadvantaged backgrounds. **This is a "must read" for all entering college freshman.**

**Dr. Victor M. Jaime**   _**Superintendent/President - Imperial Valley College**_

Reading through these articles is **like sitting down with a seasoned upperclassman or favorite academic advisor who shares their inside knowledge of how to succeed** in and make the most of the college environment.

**Dr. June E. Thompson**   _**Executive Director - California Association of Student Councils**_

Sharon's in-depth understanding of student needs and creative approach to learning makes for the ideal mix for a book aimed at guiding first-generation and under-served students through the maze that is higher education and career planning.

**Dr. Juan Avalos**   _**Vice President for Student Services - Saddleback College**_

"How To Play And Win The College Game" is an excellent resource for those students who **may not have the college know-how or cultural capital to fully understand the college experience.** This workbook provides valuable advice for those students who cannot afford to pay for a private "preparation for college program." Padilla-Alvarado uses thought-provoking questions and real-world stories of student tragedy and success to help students prepare for a transformative college experience. **An exceptional tool for anyone working with current or future college students.**

**Dr. Celia Esposito-Noy**   _**Higher Education Professional**_

Sharon Padilla-Alvarado has a special gift for understanding the nuances of a successful college experience because she lived it! I had the honor of working on the same team with Sharon at Cal Poly, San Luis Obispo. She stood out immediately amongst a group of Higher Education administrators. **I believe her keys to a successful college adventure are most likely the keys to life success. She gets it.**

**Jodi B. Gill**   _**President, The EXPERTS Bench**_

Table of Contents

"Life is a challenge, meet it! Life is a dream, realize it! Life is a game, play it..."

Sai Baba

Dedication

This book is dedicated to my family: to my parents for their endless creativity, to my husband who encouraged me to pursue my dreams, and to my children for providing a real-life example of the great potential of future generations of students. With gratitude to Doc, Patti and Joe- you made a difference in my life!

About the Author

Sharon Padilla-Alvarado is a Faculty Coordinator at Cosumnes River College (CRC) in Sacramento, California, which ranks number nine as the most diverse two year public college or university in the United States. Sharon has worked in Higher Education for over 30 years at the following colleges: California Polytechnic State University - San Luis Obispo, Sacramento State University, Imperial Valley College, Woodland Community College, Folsom Lake College, and Cosumnes River College. She has worked in the areas of Housing, Educational Equity, Student Activities, Transfer, Vocational Education, Math Engineering Science Achievement (MESA), Career Development, Academic Advising, Tutoring, and Instruction. She designed and developed the curriculum for CRC's award winning Freshman Seminar Program. Sharon earned her Bachelor of Arts Degree in Psychology and Spanish, and her Master of Arts Degree in Education, with an emphasis in Administration & Policy Analysis, from Stanford University. Sharon began working in Higher Education as an undergraduate where she held numerous internships in the Student Services Division. As a graduate student in the Stanford School of Education, she was awarded the "Dean's Award for Outstanding Service to The University." She resides with her husband and two sons in Sacramento, California.

Introduction

Congratulations! If you're reading this book you are likely enrolled in college, or you'll begin college soon. One of the great things about being in college is that you have the time to really focus on an area of study that you enjoy (your major). You may be in college 2 or 4 years, or even more if you plan on earning a graduate degree. Later on in life you'll look back at this time and realize how fortunate you were to spend quality time learning new ideas, studying, and meeting new people from so many different backgrounds and places. It makes sense to spend some time thinking and planning for a positive experience. Simple things like knowing how many classes you should take per semester, and whether or not you should work at an outside job can make a big difference in your overall experience. College also offers you the time to practice many of the skills you will need once you enter the permanent workforce. Now is a great time to take on a leadership role, learn how to work well with others, and develop the creative problem solving and decision making skills you will use throughout your career, no matter which field you choose to enter. This book will introduce you to the behaviors of successful college students (such as visiting your professors during their office hours and joining study groups) that can increase the likelihood that you will succeed and thrive in college.

Many new college students relish the freedom they have to set their own schedule, follow their interests, and manage their own money. However, for some students, all this new-found freedom can result in making costly mistakes. Most people can think of at least one student they know who did not succeed in college. Perhaps they spent too many hours partying or became overwhelmed with the cost of their college education. Or they may have spent many years studying a particular discipline, only to realize that they didn't really like that subject (and did not want to pursue a career in that area). They may have encountered academic problems that resulted in them being placed on academic probation or being dismissed from their college. How can you make sure that *you* don't become a negative statistic when it comes to earning your degree? This book can also help you to learn about common obstacles to academic success many new college students face (such as working too many hours at an outside job, or not having mentors to turn to for advice), and provide you the opportunity to plan proactively so that you steer clear of potential problems.

Spend a few hours reading through this book as part of your College Success Class or Freshman Seminar or New Student Orientation Program, or on your own to help you to understand what to expect in college and how to make the most of your college experience.

- Write in it and highlight sections that catch your attention.

- Work through the different exercises and self-assessments and think proactively about different scenarios you might encounter.

- Use the case studies and journal responses as a way to brainstorm solutions to some of the problems common to new college students.

- Share your responses with your classmates and academic counselors to get their feedback and suggestions on how to make your college experience memorable and productive.

Don't worry about figuring out everything about college your first semester. The longer you are in college, the more you will learn about how to succeed in college. Find out what works for you (e.g., early morning classes, evening classes) and try different approaches to studying, such as reviewing your notes daily, participating in a supplemental instruction group, or joining an informal study group. Be sure to assess how you did at the end of each semester, and make a mental note which strategies worked and which things you need to change to improve your odds of success. This book will help you to think about different aspects of college life- everything from how to put your class schedule together and your preferred style of learning, to how to manage your money and minimize taking on student loan debt while in college.

CHAPTER 1

College - Why You Should Play The Game

"The more that you read, the more things you know. The more that you learn, the more places you'll go."

Dr. Seuss

College – Why You Should Play the Game

Imagine you've been invited to participate in a game where, if you finish it, you're guaranteed to win $1 million! Would you be interested in playing? What if this game could significantly enhance the quality of your life- your self-esteem, your friendships, your standard of living, and your interaction with the world around you? What if, unlike most games, there was no limit to the number of winners there could be? You could win; your siblings, your friends, and your neighbors could all, also, potentially win $1 million. Would you want to play? Would you be excited about letting others know about this great game and invite them to join in?

Succeeding in college is very similar to playing a game. Games are fun; college can be great fun. Games are challenging; college is often challenging. Games have rules; colleges also have many rules (e.g., the number of units you need to earn to complete a degree or to graduate). Games have a goal; college students set many goals, such as completing their degree or program of study in a certain amount of time, or minimizing the amount of student loan debt they acquire while in college. Games often have prizes- ribbons, trophies, cash winnings, and/ or recognition. A college degree enables individuals to have access to many prizes in life- a higher paying job, choices of work options, opportunities for upward mobility, and the self-confidence and enhanced skills that come with earning a degree.

Research indicates that college graduates earn, on average, a million dollars more over their lifetime than someone with only a high school diploma. So why don't more individuals enroll in college, or complete their college program, knowing that there are significant rewards for doing so? Like many games (sports, for example) earning a college degree is a lot of work! You have to decide which game to play. You have to collect the resources needed to play the game (such as equipment or fees). You have to learn the rules of the game, and then you need to practice until you become good at the game. You have to find people who can "coach" you and cheer you on when the game gets tough. To win a game, you have to have a clear goal in mind. To complete a college degree, you have to know what you are working towards and why you are doing so. College is, in many ways, like playing a game. However, "The College Game" offers you much more than the chance to have some fun. College offers you the chance to improve your quality of life, from increasing your choices of occupations, to potentially determining which neighborhood you may be able to afford to purchase a home (which in turn may determine the schools your own children will attend, and subsequently their long term preparation for succeeding in college and the employment sector).

This book is designed to help you to learn the rules of "The College Game." By reading each chapter and completing the different worksheets and activities, you will begin to learn the behaviors of successful college students. Please write in this book! Share it with your friends, your parents, and your younger siblings who have their eye on attending college. You will find it to be a valuable resource that will help you to understand what is expected of you in college. It will enable you to understand the rules of The College Game, so you can successfully play it. I invite you to play The College Game. It is certain to be the most interesting, fun, and challenging game you have ever played.

KEY CONCEPT: The more education you have, the more money you tend to make.

What I Learned In College

If you ask someone who graduated from college a long time ago to tell you the courses they took, they'd probably have a difficult time remembering all of them. They should certainly be able to tell you what their major was, and most likely, the core courses they were required to take. Beyond that, they might have trouble remembering specifics (like exactly what they learned in each course). If I had to recreate my transcripts from memory, I'd have trouble doing so. I started out as a Psychology major (at age 18 I thought I wanted to be a psychologist), so of course, I took a lot of Psych courses. The most significant memories I have about being a Psych major are that my Introduction to Psychology professor had written THE textbook on Psychology, and there were 600 students in my Psych 1 class. I later opted for a double major in Psychology and Spanish, so I also took lots of Spanish classes. I clearly remember my Study Abroad Program, which I would say was the highlight of my college years. As part of my Spanish major, I lived in Spain for 6 months with *"chicas espanolas"* in an all-women's dorm run by nuns, and attended classes at the *Universidad de Salamanca*. I still have etched in my mind the memory of arriving in that small college town and taking in all the sights and sounds- outdoor cafés, the *plaza mayor* lit up at night, *café con leche* available 24/7, and the cobblestone streets. It almost felt as if I had arrived at Disneyland, a new, exciting place with so much to offer.

I remember some of my more difficult college courses, because they were so, well, *difficult.* I can recall struggling through some courses and not seeking help in the form of tutorial assistance, because I saw that as a sign of weakness, and how could I ever admit that I needed help?! Even if I had admitted that I occasionally needed help, I unfortunately did not know where to go on campus to seek out assistance. I remember feeling bored in some classes (e.g., I just couldn't seem to get excited about how children perceived the volume of liquids based on the shape or size of the container into which they were poured). This periodic boredom occurred even in graduate school (since theory was emphasized over practice) where I thought, "What in the world does this have to do with me, my goals, my career, and my life?" Amid thick theory-laden textbooks, I searched for practical, applicable skills that I would be able to offer the employment sector. Fortunately, I developed the real world experience and preparation I desired by holding numerous internships on campus that allowed me to practice my leadership and organizational skills.

Many of my college classes were interesting, and I found myself drawn into the material or the required texts. Despite not remembering the details of all of the courses I took, I do remember this about my college years- I had the opportunity to be around others, who like me, LOVED learning. We all trudged through our coursework, some enjoying the experience more than others, some mastering the material more easily than others. Since I lived on campus in the dorms, mealtime in the cafeteria was always something to look forward to- the real classroom, the most interesting intellectual arena. We would sit around, laughing and updating each other on what was going on in our lives (this was before anyone had ever heard of Facebook, Twitter or Instagram), while simultaneously learning from each other. At dinner I sat with the children of millionaires and the children of farmworkers at the same table. I met students from all over the world. I wish I could say that I learned a lot about my areas of specialization, but the truth is, I learned a little about a lot of things. The more I learned, the less I knew. The more I learned, the more I realized was out there for me to learn. Yet something happened between high school and college graduation. I became a better writer. I began to think more deeply, to question things. I became more confident, and I became a better public speaker. I learned to see textbooks as objects of value, as opposed to instruments of torture (something many students just out of high school think). I realized that I had opinions, and I relished sharing them through essays and written assignments. I traveled overseas and experienced living in another country. I made life-long friends. And I learned that learning never ends. While many students like to think that when they graduate from college they will be all-knowing, the truth is that the learning has only begun the day you walk across the stage to receive your college diploma. Learning is a lifelong endeavor, and college is the first step in teaching you the skills you need to keep on learning. If you ask me, "Are you glad you went to college?" the answer is a resounding "Yes!" "Was it easy?" "No!" "Was it worth it?" "Absolutely!" College is one game I'm truly glad I played.

KEY CONCEPT: Don't expect college to be like high school.

The Tabula Rasa

There is a Latin term known as the "Tabula Rasa," or the blank slate. One of the great things about college is that it provides students with a clean slate, or a new beginning—the chance to start fresh, to try something new, and even to reinvent themselves, if they want. Some college students enroll at universities far from their home town. Many students work part-time or full-time and enroll in online courses to earn their degree. Others choose to live at home while attending a community college to complete a vocational training program, or the first two years of their four year degree. Students who were not very focused in high school may decide that they are now ready to commit to putting in the time needed to succeed in college. Students who excelled in high school may choose to take a more relaxed approach to learning, now that they have been accepted to a university, and focus on enjoying their new learning environment. Others who may have not been involved in extracurricular activities while in high school may choose to avail themselves of the plethora of opportunities for extracurricular involvement on their new college campus. Whichever option you have chosen, college most likely means a new chapter in your life. As you proceed on this new journey, "don't reinvent the wheel," as the old saying goes. Learn from your past educational experience, as well as the experiences of others who have gone before you.

Think about your high school (or previous) educational experience and answer the following questions:

How committed were you in high school to academics and succeeding academically?

How committed are you in college to academic success? Has anything changed about the way you see education?

What type of behaviors helped you to succeed academically in high school?

What type of behaviors hindered your academic success in high school?

Is there anything you want to change about the way you approach your education now that you are in college?

Needs Assessment

Which of the following areas would you like to learn more about in order to get the most out of your college experience? Place a checkmark by your answers.

_____ Effective Note-taking

_____ Time Management

_____ Money Management / Paying For College

_____ Preparing For Tests

_____ Overcoming Obstacles To Academic Success

_____ Developing Leadership Skills

_____ Becoming A Critical Thinker

_____ Understanding Professors

_____ Effective Study Skills

_____ Maintaining A Healthy Self Esteem

_____ Learning Styles

_____ Academic Integrity

_____ Working Well With Others

_____ Appreciating Diversity

_____ Choosing a Major

_____ Staying Healthy In College

_____ Alcohol Awareness

_____ Transferring From A Community College To A Four Year College/University

_____ Preparing For Advanced Degrees (e.g., Graduate Degrees such as a Master's Degree or Doctorate)

What do YOU want to get out of college?

Think about where you want to go in life and what you want to achieve. You don't have to know right now exactly what you want to do with the rest of your life, but you may have already identified some general goals related to your college education.

Place a check mark next to all the answers that pertain to you:

Why are you attending college?

_____ I am in college to improve my chances of getting a job.

_____ I enrolled in classed to improve my reading, writing and/or public speaking skills.

_____ I am here to train for a career.

_____ I hope to improve my job and/or technical skills so I can be more competitive when applying for higher paying jobs.

_____ I am starting at a community college and plan to transfer to a four year college or university.

_____ I would like to earn a certificate in a vocational area.

_____ I would like to earn a four year degree.

_____ I eventually plan to apply to graduate school (I want to earn a graduate degree after earning my undergraduate degree).

_____ I really enjoy being in school and learning new things.

_____ I was given the choice by my parents to either go to school or get a job.

_____ I'm not sure what I want to do with the rest of my life and I figured this would buy me some time while I figure out what I really want to do.

_____ I signed up for classes because my friends are here.

_____ I hope to become more self-confident by earning a degree.

_____ I'm not really sure why I'm here.

_____ Other: _____

Getting Started: What Are Your Personal Goals?

There's an old saying that goes, "If you don't know where you're going, you'll probably never get there." Figuring out how you want to spend the rest of your life may take a while. Be sure to take into consideration your values and interests when selecting your academic major and career choice. If you need clarification about your interests or values, stop by your campus Career Center to see if there are any free or low cost career assessments you can take that will help you to narrow down your career choices.

Note some college majors and occupations that interest you, and which specific certificate or degree you want to earn in college.

I enjoy studying the following subjects:

_____

_____

_____

_____

I am considering the following college majors:

_____

_____

_____

_____

I am considering the following occupations/career choices:

_____

_____

_____

_____

Place a checkmark next to each item that applies to you:

____ I plan to earn a certificate in a vocational area

Name of certificate program: _____

____ I plan to earn a two year degree (A.A. or A.S.)

Name of two year degree: _____

____ I plan to earn a four year degree (B.A. or B.S.)

Name of four year degree: _____

____ I plan to transfer to a four year college or university after attending a community college in order to earn a Bachelor's Degree (B.A. or B.S.)

Where do you want to transfer? _____

Name of four year degree:

_____

____ I plan to attend graduate school after I complete a Bachelor's degree in order to earn a Master's degree/professional degree (e.g., M.B.A., Ph.D. J.D., M.D., etc.)

Which graduate university do you want to attend?

_____

Type of graduate degree:

_____

____ Other: _____

TO DO: Visit your college's Career Center to see what type of support services they offer. Review career database software available to students. Print out the details on two different careers that interest you, including a description of the careers, the educational requirements for entering these careers, the typical starting salary, and the projected outlook for new hires in this area.

Deciphering the Higher Education System

You may have felt overwhelmed in high school by all the options that were available for earning a college degree, or completing your "Post-secondary education." Now is the time to ask all the questions you have about your degree options, as different careers can require specific degrees. The segments of higher education can vary from state to state, as well as the degrees each segment offers (although you may find some overlap between their offerings). Nevertheless, you are likely to find community colleges, state universities, and private or "independent colleges" wherever you live.

If you have enrolled at a community college after high school, you will find that many courses you complete will count towards a four year degree at a university. However, many courses may not count towards transfer to a university, so it is critical that students pursuing this option work closely with Academic Counselors or Advisors to select their courses. Community college students can complete their "lower division coursework" (i.e., freshman and sophomore level courses), then complete their "upper division coursework" (i.e., junior and senior level courses) after transferring to a four year college or university. Students may also earn certificates or two year degrees (an A.A./Associate of Arts, or A.S./Associate of Science) at a community college.

If you were certain you wanted to complete a Bachelor's or four year degree (Bachelor of Arts, or Bachelor of Science), you may have chosen to enroll directly in a university after high school. The cost of enrolling can vary greatly depending on which type of university you have selected. It is important to take the cost of each college into consideration, as well as whether or not you qualify for financial aid (and how much financial aid you will receive at each campus) when deciding which college to attend. Never assume that a private college education is out of reach for you financially. While private colleges can be expensive, usually the higher the cost of tuition and other fees, the greater your chance of receiving financial aid to help cover those costs. Just because you start your degree at one college or university doesn't mean you must complete your degree there. Many students decide to switch colleges for a variety of reasons, including transferring from a community college to a four year college or university, the cost of tuition and living expenses, majors offered, and even the campus culture.

If you are interested in earning a graduate degree after completing your undergraduate studies, you may sometimes do so at the same college where you completed your Bachelor's degree. However, the application process for being accepted into graduate programs is separate from your undergraduate program. You may have to take standardized tests such as the G.R.E. (Graduate Record Exam) or the G.M.A.T. (Graduate Management Aptitude Test) and submit your scores as part of the application process. The following are examples of graduate degrees: a Master's degree (M.A., M.S., M.B.A.) or teaching credential, a law degree (J.D), or a doctorate (Ph.D., M.D.).

Don't forget that grades earned at a community college are taken into consideration when transferring to a four year college or university, as well as if you ever apply to graduate school. If you have questions about the transfer process or preparing to apply to graduate school, consult your Academic Counselor.

KEY CONCEPT: You have many choices when it comes to higher education, college degrees, and occupations.

What are you willing to sacrifice in order to succeed in college?

If you ask new college students how they feel their first year of college will go, they'll probably say they think it will go well, and that they don't anticipate any big problems. While it *is* good to think positively, too often students believe that they will sail smoothly through college without encountering *any* major difficulties. Nevertheless, many students will deal with something during their college years that will either slow them down (like flunking a class and having to retake it), or catch them off guard (such as losing a job, a friendship or relationship that ends, or dealing with an extended illness). In addition to anticipating unexpected obstacles that could slow their progress, students should also recognize that they will likely have to sacrifice something, or make some sacrifices in order to complete their college degree or goal. These sacrifices could be as simple as giving up a few weekends out with friends in order to write research papers or prepare for exams, or as big as moving across the country to attend a college with an outstanding reputation in their major. Think about how important earning a college degree is to you, and assess whether the sacrifices you are willing to make are consistent with your stated goals.

Earning my college degree is: (place a checkmark next to your answer)

_____ Extremely important

_____ Important

_____ Somewhat important

_____ Not that important

Reflect on the kinds of sacrifices you may have to make in college in order to earn your degree, then place a checkmark next to the items indicating those you would be willing to make to achieve your goal.

_____ I am willing to cut back on my work hours at an outside job so that I can focus on school.

_____ I am willing to turn down Friday evening social invitations in order to stay caught up in my classes.

_____ I am willing to turn off the TV when my favorite show is on in order to study.

_____ I am willing to give up sleeping in or going to bed early in order to study more.

_____ I am willing to turn down family social events to focus on college.

_____ I am willing to turn down Saturday evening parties in order to study.

_____ I am willing to go without new clothes this semester so that I have to work less hours at my job and can spend more time on school.

_____ I am willing cut my expenses by taking public transit or driving an older or used car, so that I have to work less at my job and will have more time to study.

_____ I am willing to break up with a significant other or stop dating for a while in order to spend more time pursuing my academic and career goals.

_____ I am willing to give up small treats like gourmet coffee drinks so that I have to work less at my job and can study more.

_____ I am willing to downsize my living arrangements in order to save money and not have to work so much while in school.

_____ I am willing to turn off my cell phone and put it in my backpack during class sessions so I can focus on the lecture or material being presented.

_____ I am willing to go an entire weekend without checking social media sites so that I can focus on academics.

_____ I am willing to turn down weekend excursions with friends in order to write a term paper or prepare for exams.

___ I am willing to come to campus on days when I do not have classes to access tutoring or other support services.

___ I am willing to refrain from attending dorm events in order to study.

___ I am willing to tell my friends I can't go out with them because I have to study.

___ I am willing to turn down working more hours at an outside job so I can focus on school.

___ I am willing to turn down a promotion at work so that I can focus on finishing my degree sooner.

___ I am willing to turn down a summer job in order to take college classes during summer session.

Add up the number of checkmarks you made and see how you scored.

15 – 20	Congratulations! You are willing to place the highest priority on your academics.
10 - 15	School is a high priority - you are willing to make many sacrifices to achieve your college goals.
5 – 10	You are willing to make some sacrifices to achieve your goals, but may need to make your academic life a higher priority.
Less than 5	Think about what is keeping you from making school a priority. Would you be willing to give up some things now in order to accomplish your academic goals? If not, why not? How could you set up your schedule so that you have a balance of personal time, money, and study time?

Journal Response:

Did you learn anything about yourself in completing this exercise? Is there anything you need to change in order to ensure your academic success?

Case Study: Hvg a gr8 time / wish u were here!

Jenny is a first year student at East Bay Community College. She earned good grades in high school and had planned to go straight to a university. However, her senior year of high school her father lost his job, so she decided to enroll in a community college and transfer later to a university to complete her Bachelor's degree. Jenny was a good student in high school, and she felt confident about her college classes, as well. She had lots of friends in high school and an active social life. The first week of school, Jenny began to think she may have made a mistake. Her friends were all off attending other colleges; she never saw the few students she knew because they had different class schedules. For the first time that she could remember, she felt lonely. When she met with an Academic Advisor regarding her class schedule, she mentioned that she felt like she was having trouble adjusting to the new environment. "Well, what did you think- that college would be like high school?!" he grumbled, as he looked out his door at the long line of students waiting to get in to see him.

After three weeks of attending class, Jenny still hasn't made any new friends. Most of the students in her classes commute to campus, and leave as soon as their classes are over. Jenny begins to feel like she is different from most of the other college students- they all seem so liberal compared to her. She is sometimes shocked by things she overhears in the cafeteria, such as other students talking in great detail about their personal lives. Jenny begins to wonder if she should drop her classes and get a job to save money so she can go to a university instead. It doesn't help that several of her friends are texting her regularly to tell her how much fun they're having at their new university campuses.

1)   Describe Jenny's feelings.

2)   Should Jenny quit attending the community college and get a job to save for attending a university later? Why or why not?

3)   Is Jenny doing anything to contribute to her feelings of isolation? If so, what?

4)   How could Jenny develop more positive feelings about the time she will spend at the community college prior to transferring to a university?

5)   What advice would you give Jenny about fitting in at her new college and making the most of her community college experience?

The True Cost Of Delaying Education

Many students think about delaying the start of college, or taking time off from college to work and save money. Keep in mind that for each extra year it takes you to complete your college degree, that's one additional year you are likely forfeiting the higher wages associated with a job in your chosen career area. Which of the following options is better? Attending four years of college and taking out $20,000 in loans to help cover your costs, or attending college half-time for eight years while working part-time, and not having to take out student loans? Imagine you  have a job waiting for you when you graduate that will pay $40,000 a year (to start). How much would you lose in wages by extending your 4 year degree to 8 years? When considering whether or not to take out student loans, be certain to calculate the amount you will have to eventually pay back once interest is added. Also find out the amount of time you will have to pay back your loans (10 years? 20 years?), as well as whether you must start making payments immediately or once you graduate from college.

Chapter Notes:

Things to think about...

Things to remember...

Things to do....

Chapter 2

Know The Rules of The Game
(The Difference Between
High School And College)

"You have to learn the rules of the game. And then you have to play better than anyone else."

Albert Einstein

Throughout this book you will find various MYTHS about college. Recent high school graduates and new college students often have these beliefs about what college or university life will be like. In reality, these are just myths. The Myths sections are designed to shed light on what you can really expect while in college.

Myth #1 - College is just like high school.

There are some similarities between high school and college, but there are many more differences. What do you think are some of the similarities? In college you have to go to class, just as in high school, and you still have to do homework and take tests. In college you may even see some of the same students who attended your high school. However, in college you are in control of how you spend your time. No one will tell you what to do, as may have happened in high school (e.g., there aren't any Hall Monitors to make you go to class). If you only want to come to school in the mornings so you can study or work in the afternoon or evening, you can probably set up your schedule that way. If you decide you don't want to do the homework or take your final exams, you can do so. Of course, you would eventually have to accept the consequences of that choice, such as flunking your classes, ending up on Academic Probation, or being dismissed from the college for having a GPA (grade point average) that is too low. In college you will not find lots of opportunities to earn extra credit, as you most likely had in high school – you either do the work and turn it in when it's due, or you don't- again it's your choice. You can expect that your college classes will be more rigorous than in high school. Whereas in high school, your teachers might have asked you to memorize lots of material and regurgitate it for tests, in college, your professors want you to really understand and interact with the material (i.e., demonstrate your critical thinking skills). So if you're taking a history class, for example, the professor probably won't ask you to memorize a bunch of dates, but rather will ask that you write a paper explaining why an event was significant, or perhaps how our society might be different today if a certain historical event did not take place.

Time Management

College provides you lots of opportunities to hone your time management skills. You most likely will have to simultaneously juggle class sessions, study time, part-time employment, and social obligations. The good news is that all this practice will prepare you for the multitude of tasks you will have to balance once you enter the permanent workforce.

Think proactively about how much you can handle at once. If you are taking 2, 3, or 4 classes *and* working at an outside job, how many hours can you realistically work without overloading yourself? If you do take on too much, something will usually have to give- your grades, your health, or your work performance on the job. Learn from your experience from previous semesters. If working 20 hours per week while being enrolled fulltime in college was way too much to do last semester, make sure you change something next semester- either the number of classes or units you take, or the number of hours you work at an outside job.

- When creating your schedule each semester, be sure to take into consideration the amount of time it will take to get from one class to another.

- Take advantage of the time between classes to study, review lecture notes for your next class, visit your professors during their office hours, or participate in extracurricular activities.

- Go to campus on days when you do not have classes in order to meet with academic counselors, use the library, participate in study groups, or access support services such as free tutoring.

- Consider cutting back on your work hours when you have a full day of classes. Try to set-up your job schedule so that you work more on days when you don't attend classes. Or, look for an on-campus job, then schedule your work hours during breaks between classes.

- Look for breaks in your schedule to attend free campus workshops on topics such as Effective Note-taking, Time Management, or Dealing With Test Anxiety.

Myth #2 - You'll have lots of free time in college. It's great because you only have to go to class a few hours a week.

Most high school students attend class about 30 hours per week. In college you can be a full-time student and be in class as few as 12 hours per week. Sounds pretty good, huh? However, it is important to note that college students can expect to study about two hours for every hour they are in class in order to "remain in good standing" (which means staying off of Academic Probation). So, in order to maintain a C average, a student taking 12 units could expect to spend another 24 hours per week studying for those classes (i.e., reading textbooks, reviewing notes, or preparing for exams). Some classes will require even more time; some will require less. If you want to earn "A" grades in all your classes, you can expect to spend even more time studying each week. But on the average, you should plan on 2 hours for every hour you are in class. If you attend a community college and want to transfer to a university in 2 years, you will most likely take at least 15 units each semester. So, you can count on about 30 hours a week that you will need to study outside of class. You can see how enrolling in 12-15 college units is similar to having a full-time job. Lots of students don't realize that they will need so much time to do their college work, so they think they can hold an outside job for 20 or 30 hours per week. Students who end up on Academic Probation usually have too much on their plate- they're taking too many units, working too many hours at an outside job, attending too many social functions, and/or are not putting in enough study hours.

KEY CONCEPT: Know the rules of the game- pay attention to deadlines, policies, and procedures.

Throughout this book you will find many "FAQ's" or Frequently Asked Questions. These are typical questions new students have about enrolling in courses, the college environment, and how to succeed in college.

FAQ: How many hours can I work while in college and still maintain good grades?

Every college unit or credit you enroll in represents approximately one hour of class time. So if you enroll in 12 units, you can expect to be in class about 12 hours per week, and spend about 24 hours per week outside of class time studying, completing homework assignments, and preparing for exams. Some classes may take more time, and some may take less, but on average you can expect to spend two hours studying per week for each hour you are in class. Being a full-time college student really is like having a full-time job! You must therefore plan accordingly when balancing your college courses and outside employment. Many students work part-time (8 – 15 hours per week) and are still able to take a full course load. Overloading your schedule with too many commitments will set you up for failure. Plan ahead, and cut back on your work hours or the number of units you enroll in each term, as necessary. You'll be glad you did, and you'll most likely earn better grades, be less stressed out, and have an overall better college experience.

KEY CONCEPT: Don't try to take on too much at once. Know how many units you can handle. Find out which class, study and job schedules work best for you.

Developing A Weekly Schedule

On the blank weekly schedule (following page) note all the commitments you have each week.

1) Block off the hours you will be in class this semester. If you are taking 12 units, block off an additional 24 hours of outside study time. If you are taking 15 units, block off 30 hours a week of outside study time. Build some time into your schedule for commuting or getting to class. Add in the time it takes you to get to and from class (especially if you commute to campus).

2) If you have a job, block off the hours you are at work. Be sure to include the time it takes to commute to and from your job. If you are attending college fulltime, it is best not to work more than 15 hours per week at an outside job. If you attend college part-time, you may be able to work 20 or more hours per week at an outside job; this may depend on how well-prepared you are academically for college, and how demanding your courses are in any given semester.

3) Calculate the amount of time you need to sleep, to eat and for personal matters; note this on your schedule.

4) If you live at home with your parents/family, block off the amount of time you need to do household chores or to attend family functions.

5) Determine how much time you have leftover each week for recreation (e.g., going out with friends, playing Intramural Sports, joining student clubs, etc.). Designate some time for non-school and non-work activities, such as exercising or meeting with friends to make sure you stay healthy physically and emotionally.

6) If in doing this exercise you have more activities posted than you have hours in the day, look at your weekly schedule to see where you can cut back. Can you take out a student loan instead of working so many hours at an outside job? Can you live closer to campus so that you spend less time commuting to and from classes? Will you need to cut back on social activities in order to have sufficient study time? Take the time to plan a realistic schedule early each semester to ensure you're not taking on too much.

My Weekly Schedule

	Mon	Tues	Weds	Thurs	Fri	Sat/Sun
5 a.m.						
6 a.m.						
7 a.m.						
8 a.m.						
9 a.m.						
10 a.m.						
11 a.m.						
12 p.m.						
1 p.m.						
2 p.m.						
3 p.m.						
4 p.m.						
5 p.m.						
6 p.m.						
7 p.m.						
8 p.m.						
9 p.m.						
10 p.m.						
11 p.m.						
12 a.m.						

Myth #3 - It doesn't matter if you show up to class – no one will notice...

While it is true that some faculty never take attendance, especially in large lecture classes, many do routinely take roll. If you're sitting in a lecture hall with 600 students in the same class, your professor most likely will not keep track of who attends. However, the smaller the class, the more likely the professor will take attendance, which could influence your grade. So be sure not to miss those small discussion classes!

Most instructors will state their attendance policy on their syllabus. Make sure you know each professor's policies. It's a good idea to notify your professors via email if you're going to miss more than one class session for extenuating circumstances, such as illness or a family emergency.

There are some college students who are able to miss lots of class sessions, read the textbook, and still get A's in their classes. However, the majority of students aren't so lucky. You really have to be present at each class session to hear the lecture, take notes, interact with classmates, know what to expect on tests, and to later be able to work on group projects and participate in study groups.

If you consider the overall cost of your college education, missing a class is like pouring money down the drain. To find out how much each lecture hour is worth on average, divide the annual cost of your college education by 384 (the approximate number of hours you would attend class if you are enrolled full-time—12 units x 2 semesters x 16 weeks). If you are attending a private university where overall costs can run over $50,000 per year, missing one hour of class is like losing over $100. When you take this into consideration, it makes sense to only miss class for serious reasons (such as illness).

For more reasons why you shouldn't miss class, see the article in Chapter 5 entitled "Your Professor Called- She Can't Start Class Without You."

To get a better idea of what professors expect from you, see the exercise in this chapter entitled "Inappropriate Behavior."

Deciphering Academic Publications

While in college you will have several publications available to you that outline your various options for completing a degree or meeting your academic goals.

- Be sure to purchase a copy of your college's **Catalog** at the campus bookstore, or know how to access the online version of this important document on your college's website.

- **Class Schedules** will vary from semester to semester; these are available online, and sometimes in print at your college Counseling Center or Campus Bookstore. Class Schedules list all the courses that are being taught the next term, the days and times the classes meet, the instructor's name, and other information relevant to registering for classes, such as course codes. Class Schedules can change quickly as new classes are added or courses become fully enrolled, so be sure to check this resource frequently as you approach registering for courses for each upcoming semester or quarter.

- Spend some time familiarizing yourself with your college's **website**. You will find tons of valuable information such as deadlines for adding and dropping classes, phone numbers and office locations of important campus resources, and even hints for how to deal with test anxiety or how to stay safe on campus.

College Terminology You Need To Know

There are many words that are specific to a college or university environment. Even before you enroll in classes you will begin to hear these words, such as Lower or Upper Division courses, General Education Requirements, Prerequisites, and (if you start your education at a community college) Articulation Agreements. If you hear words being used that you don't know, jot them down and look them up as soon as possible, as you are likely to hear these words repeatedly. You can ask your Academic Advisor or students who have been in college for a while to explain any terms that are unclear. Your college catalog is also a great place to look up new terms (see a handy list of topics covered by checking the Index located in the back of the catalog).

Adding / Dropping – Students sometimes "Add" or "Drop" classes after the initial registration period (i.e., they either try to enroll in a class, or they drop a class in which they already enrolled). During the first week of classes each semester or quarter, many students Add or Drop courses- this is quite common. There are usually deadlines for Adding or Dropping classes. Some colleges will require you to show proof that the instructor is allowing you to Add into a class (e.g., use a permission number that s/he gives you so you can register for the class). At some colleges, if you stop attending a class but fail to file a Drop Card with the Registrar's Office, you may end up receiving an "F" grade at the end of the semester for that course. Never assume that an instructor will drop you from a class if you just stop attending. It is fairly easy to Drop a class, but may be difficult to Add a class, as there are only so many seats for students in each class section, and usually many students wanting to Add into each class.

Articulation Agreements – These are formal agreements between different colleges outlining course equivalencies (e.g., Psych 1, Intro. to Psychology, at one college may be the same as Psych 100, General Psychology at another). Some colleges enter into agreements with other colleges acknowledging students moving from one institution to the other will receive credit for specific courses. Students who transfer from a community college to a university will need to review and carefully plan their coursework around formal articulation agreements.

Class Schedule – Each college has a schedule of classes prepared in advance for each term that is generally available in print or online. Consult the Class Schedule to figure out the times, days, and start and end dates of classes you want to take. The Class Schedule also lists the instructor for each section, and whether the class will last the full semester or quarter, or whether it will last a lesser number of weeks.

College Catalog – This is the official document that outlines each college's policies, procedures, degrees and course offerings, etc. The requirements for your major will most likely be outlined in detail here. This is like a contract between the university and you where the requirements you will be held to in order to earn specific degrees or certificates are outlined.

Credit / No Credit – You may have the option to take some courses Credit / No Credit, which means you either pass the class (and get "Credit" posted on your transcript) or you don't pass (and you get "No Credit" posted on your transcript). This is in place of a letter grade. You may want to take some courses Credit / No Credit so you can focus on learning the material, and not on the grade you receive. Students are generally not allowed to take courses in their major Credit / No Credit. A Credit grade is usually calculated as a C in your Grade Point Average (GPA). If you plan to apply to graduate school, you'll want to minimize the number of courses you take Credit/No Credit, as these can affect your GPA.

Electives – You must complete a certain number of units to earn your college degree. Some of your units will come from your major courses, some from required General Education courses, and some from courses required for graduation. Students generally have some additional units they can complete towards their degree in elective courses. These classes can usually be in any area. Electives provide you with the opportunity to take additional courses in your major, or in another area that interests you.

General Education – These are courses all students are required to take to complete a two year or four year college degree. You can expect to have to take courses in English Composition, math, science, and humanities, in addition to those required for your major. These are required to ensure that students have a well-rounded education, and that they are exposed to material from courses across the curriculum.

GPA – This is the average of your grades based on points assigned to each letter. A student with a 4.0 GPA would have earned all A's in his or her classes. A student with all B's would have a 3.0 GPA, etc. To receive academic honors or to avoid being place on Academic Probation, students need to maintain a specific GPA (usually higher than a C or 2.0).

Incompletes – If you don't finish all the requirements for a particular class, the professor may give you an "Incomplete" grade which allows you some extra time to finish up the requirements. This is usually prearranged with the professor, and there is a time limit that you have to complete the pending work. Instructors may be willing to give you an Incomplete if you become ill towards the end of the semester and miss numerous class sessions, or have some other serious emergency.

Index – The Index can usually be found at the back of your College Catalog. It consists of an alphabetized list of the contents of the catalog and the page numbers where each topic can be found. When you need to reference something in your catalog, such as Graduation Requirements, checking the Index will save you a lot of time.

Lower Division / Upper Division – Lower Division courses are those offered at the Freshman and Sophomore level. Upper Division courses are those offered at the Junior and Senior level. Students generally complete their Lower Division courses prior to taking Upper Division courses. Community colleges offer Lower Division courses. Four year universities offer both Lower Division and Upper Division courses.

Major / Minor / Double Major – A Major is your main program of study, such as Biology or History. A Minor is when you complete a specific number of units (approximately 20) in a secondary area. A Double Major is when students choose to complete the requirements for two different majors. Students completing a Double Major usually only complete one set of General Education and/or Graduation Requirements.

Part-time / Full-time – Part-time students take less than 12 units per semester. Full-time students usually take 12 – 15 or more units per semester. If you receive Financial Aid, you must be enrolled full-time to receive 100% of your aid. If you are enrolled half-time (6 units), you will likely only receive half of the Financial Aid you are eligible for any given semester.

Prerequisite / Co-requisite – A Prerequisite is a course you must take before you can enroll in a subsequent course (e.g., you must take Algebra before Advanced Algebra). A Co-requisite is a course that you must take at the same time as another course (e.g., you may have to take a Physics Lab course at the same time as the Physics course).

Semester System / Quarter System– Most colleges and universities operate on the Semester System. They offer Fall and Spring Semester each year. Schools on the Quarter System offer three sessions each year – Fall, Winter and Spring Quarters. Students enrolled in either system generally can register for classes during Summer Session/Quarter, as well.

Syllabus – On the first day of class each professor distributes his or her course syllabus. This is an outline of what will be covered in the class. Contact information for how to reach the professor (e.g., email address, office hours, office location), the due dates for upcoming assignments, his or her grading policies, the date of upcoming exams, and textbooks you are required to purchase will also be listed here. The syllabus is like a contract between the professor and the students; it states what will be covered in the course and details classroom policies. It is a good idea to place your syllabus at the front of a separate binder or notebook you have for each class. Professors often post their course syllabus online for easy access.

Transcript- This is the college's official record of your grades. You can usually go online and view (and print out) unofficial copies of your transcripts. You can also order official transcripts which are sent directly from the college Registrar's Office to graduate schools where you are seeking admission, or to outside agencies reviewing scholarship applications.

Undergraduate / Graduate Student – An Undergraduate student is working on a degree such as an Associate of Arts or Associate of Science (2 year degree) or a Bachelor of Arts or Bachelor of Science (4 year degree). Students who enroll in coursework beyond the Undergraduate level are considered Graduate Students. "Grad" students include students enrolled in Master's, Ph.D., and professional school programs such as medical or law school.

College Terminology Exercise

Match the following words to the correct definition:

___ Associate's Degree	___ Bachelor's Degree	___ College Catalog
___ Class Schedule	___ General Education	___ Graduate Degrees
___ G.P.A.	___ Prerequisite	___ Lower Division
___ Semester	___ Syllabus	___ Upper Division

A. The average of one's grades.

B. A publication outlining all of the college's policies, regulations, and degree offerings.

C. An online and/or printed publication that comes out before the start of each new term. This lists the courses offered the upcoming semester or quarter, as well as the days and times different class sections will meet.

D. A two year degree that can be earned at a community college.

E. Freshman and Sophomore level courses are referred to as:

F. This term usually lasts 16 – 18 weeks.

G. A course that must be completed prior to enrolling in another course.

H. A four year degree offered by a college or university.

I. M.A., M.S., M.B.A., Ph.D., J.D., M.D.

J. An outline of course requirements distributed by professors on the first day of class. This can be available as a hard copy or an online document.

K. Junior and Senior level courses are referred to as:

L. Courses students are required to take as part of their degree program, often outside of one's major.

FAQ: What are prerequisite courses and why do I have to take them?

Simply stated, prerequisite courses must be taken before subsequent courses. For example, some colleges won't let students take Advanced German until they have taken Intermediate German (or can prove that they are sufficiently fluent in German to succeed in an advanced course). Prerequisite requirements ensure that students take sequential courses in the proper order. They also guarantee that students have covered a specific body of material, and that they have achieved certain levels of competency before they attempt more complex or advanced material.

Sometimes completion of prerequisites is verified or enforced by the college at the time of registration, or by the professor. Prerequisite courses are generally noted in the Class Schedule or College Catalog. Sometimes professors will announce at the first class session the prerequisite courses students should have completed prior to starting that particular course. Some colleges don't enforce completion of prerequisites and rely on students to self-regulate and only enroll in courses for which they are prepared. It is in your best interest to adhere to prerequisite course requirements in order to be sufficiently prepared to succeed in each subsequent course. It may be tempting to skip English Composition or other courses to go into higher level courses that are required for your major. However, the prerequisites are there for a reason, and even if your college professors don't find out that you skipped required prerequisite courses, you most likely will encounter difficulty in the more advanced courses because of missing knowledge or skills. In the case where you do not want to complete a prerequisite course because you have sufficient knowledge of the subject or expertise in the field, you can sometimes request to take a challenge exam to prove competency in the subject matter or to earn credit by exam.

Why You Should Read Your College Catalog

Would you start out on a road trip to a new place without first obtaining a map of where you're going for the easiest route to get there? Probably not! It makes sense that before you invest time and money in your college education, you should take some time to plan your route. Your College Catalog has tons of valuable information on how to map out your educational pathway. Reviewing your College Catalog is similar to logging onto the Internet to access MapQuest or other sources for obtaining directions; like a GPS, it can tell you the best (and quickest) way to get from Point A to Point Z.

A quick overview of your College Catalog can help you to better understand the following topics:

- The Academic Calendar for the Fall and Spring semesters and Summer Session, as well as major deadlines and school holidays.

- Freshman and Transfer Admissions requirements and procedures.

- A list of programs of study or majors, as well as degrees and certificates that are offered.

- Detailed descriptions of courses, including prerequisites.

- Lists of courses that are transferable to other major college/university systems.

- Graduation requirements.

- The availability of student support services, such as Tutoring, Counseling, Library Services, Financial Aid, and more, to help you with career decision-making, problem resolution and goal achievement.

The best place to start when looking up information in your college catalog is the **Index**, which is located at the back of the publication. Topics are listed in alphabetical order, making whatever you're looking for easy to find- everything from Academic Regulations to Work Experience (Internship) opportunities. Spend some time perusing your College Catalog and keep it close to

your work area (or bookmark it on your computer), as you will want to consult it routinely throughout your college career.

Maintaining Catalog Rights

If you enroll in a college and then stop attending for a period of time (e.g., more than 1 – 2 semesters), you may find that your college will not allow you to abide by the degree requirements listed in the college catalog at the time you enrolled, but will make you adhere to the requirements listed in a more recent catalog (the one that is in effect at the time you re-enroll). Students should become familiar with their college's policy regarding catalog rights, and avoid taking extended breaks from enrolling in classes. Having to work with a different catalog may mean you have to complete additional requirements that have been added to your major or academic program since you first started college. If you start your education at a community college and then transfer to a four year college or university, you will also want to pay attention to catalog rights. If you have questions about maintaining your catalog rights, consult an Academic Counselor at your campus.

KEY CONCEPT: Students who study in groups (or with others) tend to do better academically than students who study alone.

Deciphering Academic Publications Exercise

Refer to your College or University Catalog, Schedule of Classes, and college website to answer the following questions. (Answer questions #1 & #2 only if you are enrolled in a community college.)

1) True or false? Once you earn an A.A. or A.S. degree from a community college, you can automatically transfer to a 4 year university.

2) If you attend a community college, how can you tell if your course credits will transfer to a four year institution (i.e., count towards a Bachelor's degree)?

3) What is the minimum GPA (grade point average) you need to graduate from your college or university with a degree?

4) List five types of information you can find in your College Catalog:

5) Do you automatically get a refund if you drop a class, or are you required to complete and submit a form?

6) What is the name of the office at your college or university that provides career advice and support to students?

7) In order to earn your degree, how many units will you need to complete (minimum)?

8) What is the name of the back portion of your college catalog that lists where different information is located?

9) How far in advance do you have to register for classes for each coming semester or term?

Inappropriate Classroom Behavior

Although your professors may not state directly on their syllabus how they expect their students to conduct themselves, they definitely have a clear idea of the kinds of things that students do that bother them. Stay in your professors' good graces by making sure you're not guilty of any of these offensive behaviors!

If you were to poll your college professors to find out what types of behaviors they do not want to see in their classes, their responses would probably be similar to this list.

Of the following behaviors, select the five that you think are MOST likely to irritate your professors (rank in order 1 – 5).

____ Arriving late to class

____ Arriving without paper or pens/pencils to take notes

____ Leaving class early (without having cleared it first with the instructor)

____ Missing classes (without notifying the instructor if an emergency has come up)

____ Asking the instructor (after you missed a class), "Did I miss anything?"

____ Signing in on the roll sheet for a friend who is absent, or having a friend sign in for you even though you're absent

____ Turning in homework late

____ Disrupting the class (being noisy, goofing off, talking about something other than the class material)

____ Text-messaging your friends

____ Surfing the Internet during lectures

____ Not turning off your cell phone prior to the start of class

____ Eating in class

____ Talking to classmates during a lecture

___ Taking a phone call during a class session

___ Stepping outside of the classroom during class to take or make a phone call

___ Leaving class for a brief period

___ Arguing with the instructor or classmates in a manner that is counterproductive to the learning environment

___ Not doing the assigned reading ahead of time

___ Working on homework during class

___ Packing up your backpack or briefcase before class ends

When in doubt regarding your professors' expectations:

- Check the syllabus for specific rules or policies your instructor may have about classroom behavior.

- If you think a particular behavior may offend your instructor or classmates, play it safe and don't do it!

Journal Assignment:

Elaborate on the top five behaviors you selected. Why do you think these would bother your professors more than the other behaviors? Have you ever been guilty of doing any of these things in class? If so, what can you do to make sure you don't do this in the future (so you can stay on good terms with your instructors *and* get the most from your classes)?

Case Study: Insufficient Funds

The week before his college classes started, Eric went to the Bookstore to buy the textbooks he needed. Since he only had to buy 4 books, he figured it wouldn't be too expensive. However, when he added up the cost of the books, he was shocked to find that he owed $643.00 plus tax. Since he only had three hundred dollars in his checking account, he decided to pay with his credit card. He had heard he could save money by buying used textbooks, but since this was his first semester in college, he decided he'd treat himself, and opted for new books. "Besides," he thought, "who wants to read books someone else has already marked up?!" When it was his turn to pay the cashier, he handed over his credit card, only to hear the cashier say "I'm sorry, sir. Your credit card was denied. You'll have to make some other form of payment." Eric felt himself break into a sweat, and wished the clerk had spoken in a lower voice. He was sure the students in line behind him had overheard what she said. He realized he must have reached the limit on his credit card when he took his girlfriend out to that nice restaurant and to a movie last weekend. He knew he only had $300 in his account, but he was expecting a Financial Aid check to arrive in the mail any day now. Payday was still one week away. He figured he'd be able to pay down the balance on his credit card and cover the amount he needed for textbooks once these checks were deposited in his bank account. The cashier stated again, even louder than before, "Sir, you'll need to come up with some other form of payment." He glanced at a sign near the cash register that read "$100 fee for returned checks." Just then his cell phone rang. He could tell it was his girlfriend, and he knew she was calling him to discuss their plans for the upcoming weekend. She was a year younger than him and was starting her senior year in high school. She had been concerned lately that he was going to "dump" her for some coed once he started college. He had tried to reassure her that their relationship was secure by buying her a pair of earrings and spending more time with her. He decided to let the call go to voice mail. "Sir," the cashier stated, "if you can't pay for your books, you'll have to return them to the shelves." He hesitated for a moment, then reached for his checkbook.

1)   What is the biggest problem Eric is facing?

2)   What are some other issues he must address?

3)   What are some ways Eric could save money?

4)   What advice would you give Eric about dealing with his girlfriend?

Self-Assessment

Rate yourself on the behaviors of successful students on a scale of 1 – 5. How well prepared are you in the following areas?

    1 = I need lots of help with this

    2 = I could do better in this area

    3 = I'm OK in this area

    4 = I do a good job in this area

    5 = I'm very good at this

ACADEMIC EXCELLENCE

_____ I know how to interpret my scores on Math and English Placement Exams

_____ I pay attention to prerequisite requirements for different courses

_____ I know how to calculate my GPA

_____ I know what my professors expect and what they would consider inappropriate behavior in class

_____ I attend campus workshops on topics such as Study Skills and How To Select A Major

_____ I enroll in courses that will help me to be successful in college such as a Freshman Seminar or College Success class

_____ I am willing to organize a study group for students in my classes if one does not exist

_____ I know the deadline for adding and dropping classes each term

_____ I know what is required to make the Dean's Honor Roll at my college

_____ I know how to stay off of Academic Probation

___ I know how to make the most of the General Education courses I must take as part of my degree

___ I know how to earn college credit by taking Advanced Placement classes in high school and by getting credit by exam

___ I understand my options should I decide to pursue graduate school

Place a checkmark next to any items that you rated a 1 (I need lots of help with this) or a 2 (I could do better in this area). Identify where you could go on campus in order to solicit help and learn more about these areas.

The following resources can help you to learn more about how to excel in college.

- You Academic Advisor can answer questions about placement test scores, prerequisite requirements, General Education requirements, AP credit, degree options beyond a four year degree, and calculating your Grade Point Average.

- Take advantage of free campus workshops on different topics such as Effective Study Skills, or sign up for a College Success or Study Skills class early in your college career.

- You College Catalog is a valuable resource for learning what it takes to graduate with honors and avoid academic probation.

Chapter Notes:

Things to think about...

Things to remember...

Things to do....

Chapter 3

Have a Game Plan

"Instead of thinking about where you are, think about where you want to be. It takes twenty years of hard work to become an overnight success."

Diana Rankin

Choosing a Major

At some point in your college career you are going to have to declare your major, or main program of study. You may already know which major you want to pursue your first semester in college; however, it's OK if you haven't decided on a major when you start college. Many students are undecided about their major and take several semesters to narrow down their choice. Some colleges even allow students to be an "Undeclared Major" for a period of time. You may find yourself having to choose from several different majors that interest you. You might also find yourself debating between a major that you know will enable you to get a job once you graduate from college, or one that you find more interesting and rewarding on a personal level (your passion).

If you are in need of information in order to select a major, schedule some time to meet with Academic Advisors in different departments to discuss your interests, and to learn more about the requirements for different majors, as well as the career options for various majors. Although every major has mandatory courses you must complete, you will usually have some leeway in selecting elective courses to complete the total number of units required for your major. You will also need to decide which General Education (G.E.) courses to take. General Education requirements ensure that students are well-rounded when they graduate and are knowledgeable about a variety of subjects. Science majors will find that they are required to take some credits in the Humanities (e.g., foreign language) and Social Sciences (e.g., Psychology or Sociology), and Humanities majors will find that they must complete some courses in Math and Science (e.g., Statistics, Physics, or Chemistry). Students can also expect to take courses in English to develop their writing skills, as well as courses in Oral Communication to ensure they are competent in public speaking.

If you are undecided about a major, spend some time taking General Education classes while you investigate your options. You may find that you enjoy a particular G.E. area so much that you decide to select it as your major. Just because you major in Economics or Accounting does not necessarily mean that you are committing to a lifelong career in banking or working for an accounting firm. Of course, a degree in Economics or Accounting will better prepare you for working in these industries (as well as make you more marketable in these fields) than, perhaps, a degree in Molecular Biology or Theatre Arts. If you ask others who have graduated from college whether they work in an area closely related to their college major, you will most likely find many who do, as well as many others with jobs or career paths that are quite different from what they studied in college. Luckily, in college you are able to develop skills that can be utilized in a variety of fields. So don't worry that your college degree or major will lock you into one job or career path for the rest of your life. If you have questions about the types of jobs you can apply for once you finish college, talk to people working in the fields that interest you and ask them for their recommendation on different majors. Also consider stopping by your college's Career Center to see if they offer free or low cost Career Interest Inventories that can help you to decide which career field you want to enter. Your college Career Center will most likely have Career Counselors that are available to assist you with obtaining information and narrowing down your choices. They can also help you to obtain internships in your field so you have a chance to test the waters before you enter the permanent workforce.

Many universities allow students to create their own major. This is a great option for students who find that they are interested in several different academic areas, but can't quite narrow down their choice to one single subject. In order to create a special major you will need to research the requirements for doing so in your college catalog. You will likely submit a proposal to university officials outlining which courses you would like to take and how you will benefit (e.g., career-wise) from this unique arrangement of courses. You will also need to demonstrate how your major is different from all other existing majors at your college or university, and that it is interdisciplinary in nature (i.e., it includes courses from a variety of academic areas).

Choosing A Major Exercise

Sometimes if you aren't sure what you want to do career-wise, it is helpful to identify some careers you know you don't want to enter, as well as what it is about those career choices that you consider unappealing (e.g., "I don't want to work in an office setting because I prefer to work in an environment with lots of physical activity"). List four career occupations you know you <u>definitely do not want to enter</u>, as well as the reasons each option doesn't appeal to you:

<u>CAREER / OCCUPATION</u>   <u>Reasons why I dislike this option:</u>

1)

2)

3)

4)

While our choices of desirable occupations may change over time, frequently we can see some type of pattern related to our career preferences (e.g., "I have often thought about being a teacher, a nurse, or a psychologist, and each of these occupations involves helping others").

Fill in the blanks:

When I was a child, I wanted to be a _____ when I grew up.

In high school, I thought I would be a _____ when I grew up.

Now that I am in college I am thinking about entering the following careers:

_____

_____

_____

Do you see any common characteristics in the occupations you have considered throughout your life? If so, note what they have in common:

List three TRADITIONAL majors that people who typically enter your preferred career might select when in college (e.g., someone considering a career as a Pharmacist would typically major in Biology, Chemistry, or another science area).

1)

2)

3)

Now identify three NONTRADITIONAL majors you could select in order to enter your preferred career. If you can't think of a nontraditional major for your occupation, ask your instructor, counselor, or classmates- chances are they know someone who entered your career field who did not take the traditional route.

1)

2)

3)

Review the six majors you listed in the previous two questions, and rank order your preference. That is, which one most appeals to you the most, which one would you select as a second choice, etc.? Note: this doesn't mean you have to select any of these majors! This is just an exercise to get you to reflect on some possible options for your college major.

1)

2)

3)

4)

5)

6)

In order to enter you preferred career area or occupation, how much college will you need to complete? If you do not know the answer to this, stop by your college Career Center and review their job and career databases.

   ___   a)   some technical training

   ___   b)   a two year degree

   ___   c)   a four year degree

   ___   d)   a four year degree plus a graduate degree

If you selected D, what type of graduate degree will you need to earn?

   ___   Master's degree

   ___   Ph.D.

   ___   M.D.

   ___   J.D.

   ___   M.B.A.

   ___   other (please list)_____

Are there any other licenses or certificates you will need in order to enter your preferred occupation, in addition to a degree(s)? If you do not know the answer to this question, check with someone who is already working in that career, or consult the career databases in your college's Career Center.

Journal Assignment:

You may be enrolled in college anywhere from 2 – 4 years or more. What do you want to accomplish during this time besides earning a certificate or degree? How do you hope to change personally, professionally or in other ways? What personal traits do you want to develop? What kinds of professional skills do you want to gain?

Myth #4: Successful students never change their major.

If you want to upset your parents, call them every few months and tell them you've changed your major (again)! While this might temporarily stress them out, it is actually very common for students to change their major. Don't feel like you absolutely need to know your major the first day you start college. It may take you a while to figure out what you want to study. In the meantime, there are lots of General Education classes that you can take that are required as part of your degree (all students take General Education courses as part of a two or four year degree program). Your first year or two of college are also a good time to take intro-level classes that appeal to you, particularly if you are interested in many areas and are having trouble narrowing down a major. You can also enroll in the Cooperative Education or Work Experience Program, if it is offered at your college or university, which enables you to earn academic credit for completing a paid or volunteer internship in a specific field. It's better to try a job in a field that you're considering and realize early on it's not exactly what you want, than to spend four or more years studying a subject, only to realize you don't really want to work in that field. An internship can help you to confirm that you have selected the right major and career path, and enable you to make valuable professional contacts you can tap after graduation. You might consider doing a double major, or a major and a minor if you're interested in more than one area. You do need to be careful that you don't switch your major too often or too late in the game, or your 4 year degree can easily turn into a 6 or 8 year degree.

KEY CONCEPT: It pays to get organized. Plan for success.

FAQ: What if I can't decide between two majors?

If you're interested in more than one major, you have various options. Consider declaring a "double major" (e.g., Business and History, or Computer Science and a foreign language) so that you can study more than one discipline. In this case, you would most likely complete one set of General Education courses and Graduation Requirements, as well as the core course requirements for two majors. It may be possible to complete a double major without adding any extra semesters to your Bachelor's degree program; instead of taking numerous elective courses to earn enough units to graduate, you would take the required courses for a second major. Be sure to check with your college's Graduation or Registrar's Office to find out whether you will earn two separate undergraduate degrees, or one degree in two majors. Another option you can consider is selecting your first choice as your major, and enrolling in additional courses to complete a "minor" in another academic area. Or, if you would like to take additional courses in another area, you can sometimes do this as part of your General Education or to fulfill Graduation Requirements; you can do this without declaring a second major or a minor.

HINTS:

- If you're undecided about a major, focus on completing your General Education requirements, and experiment by taking some intro-level courses in majors you are considering.

- If you're having trouble deciding between two majors, consider completing a double major- one that you know will enable you to find employment after graduation, and one that you select because you enjoy the subject matter.

- If you were to design your own major, which courses would you include and why? See if your college or university will allow you to design your own major.

**KEY CONCEPT: It's OK not to know right now
what you want to do with the rest of your life.**

Major & Career Connections- Exercise

Brainstorm a list of 20 careers or jobs you can do with a major in:

_____

(insert name of your major here)

For example, a student who majors in Culinary Arts could compete for the following jobs:

Restaurant Owner, Line Cook, Grocery Store Manager, Baker, Cook in a school or private business, Cafeteria Manager, Hotel Employee, Caterer, Personal Chef, etc.

Organize the jobs you listed into major categories (e.g., the jobs listed above could fall in to the following categories: food preparation, management, business enterprise, etc.).

From the list of 20 jobs you brainstormed, select the top 3 that interest you the most. Why are these more appealing to you?

TO DO:

Find three people you know who earned a college degree that ended up working in a career outside of their major field or area (e.g., a Graphic Communications major who now works in banking or real estate). Ask them the following questions:

- What skills did you learn or develop as a result of your major that you were able to apply in your current job setting?

- What are some other jobs you've had (or considered) that were outside of your academic major?

- Did you have to return to school/college for further training to assume this job?

Supplies Checklist

Before your classes start each semester, stop by your campus bookstore or local office supply store and purchase any items you will need. Use the following list to see what you already have and what you still need to purchase; add to this list as necessary.

_____ Binders (use a different one for each class)

_____ Three-hole punched binder paper

_____ Spiral binders for taking notes

_____ A weekly planner or wall calendar

_____ Computer programs or phone apps that enable you to monitor your schedule

_____ A stapler and a box of staple refills

_____ Blank index cards in different colors and sizes

_____ Number #2 pencils, pens in different colors, and a good eraser

_____ A pre-paid card for printing or making photocopies on campus

_____ A good Dictionary & Thesaurus

Other supplies you may need:

_____ A backpack (a rolling one if you anticipate carrying around lots of heavy books)

_____ *A calculator

_____ Reams of printing paper and extra ink cartridges for your computer printer

_____ A three-hole punch

_____ Dividers in different colors (or numbered/alphabetized inserts) for binders

_____ Paper Clips

_____ *Blue Books & SCANTRON Forms for taking exams

_____ Flash Drives

_____ Colored pencils or multi-colored pens (these are great for organizing your notes)

_____ Highlighters in different colors for outlining your textbooks or notebooks

*See your class syllabi for recommendations from instructors on what type you should purchase

FAQ: What happens if I need to take some Developmental Courses in math or English?

It's not the end of the world if you have to take one or more developmental (also known as basic skills) courses. Lots of students need to brush up on their math or writing skills before they attempt college level courses in these areas. What's important to note is that basic skills courses generally do not count towards your degree. So the more developmental courses you have to take, the longer it will take you to complete your degree or to meet your educational

goal. Students enrolled at community colleges will need to complete any pre-college level courses prior to transferring to a four year college or university. Students enrolled at a four year campus are often given one year to finish any remedial work needed. If at the end of their first year they are not ready for college level math or English courses, they may be required to enroll in a community college for a while to focus on developing these skills prior to returning to their four year college or university.

Academic Advising

Most colleges employ Academic Counselors or Advisors to assist students with things such as figuring out the requirements to earn a specific degree, how to put a class schedule together, and (if you are enrolled at a community college) how to transfer to a four year college or university. It is definitely worth the time you spend meeting with your advisor, as they can help you to make sure you take only required courses. Taking courses that aren't required may be money down the drain (unless you purposely choose to take them in addition to your required courses because they offer you valuable skills or knowledge you will need later on in your life or career).

FAQ: How do I know which classes to take? Can I trust my Academic Counselor to give me accurate information?

Although the majority of academic counselors or advisors do provide excellent information, it is important to understand that they are human, and they can (and sometimes do) make mistakes. With each advisor potentially being responsible for advising 900-1000 different students per year, it is possible that they might overlook a requirement you need to graduate. Finding out in the middle of your last semester that you are still missing one or two classes to graduate is sure to make you want to tear your hair out. It is imperative that you check and double-check everything your Academic Advisor tells you against your college or university catalog. Sometimes it is helpful to check with more than one advisor, especially if something seems amiss in the information you have been given. This is especially true for students who are planning on transferring from one college to another; be sure to consult formal Articulation Agreements between your community college and the university where you plan to transfer (these may be available through online databases such as the ASSIST database in California, www.ASSIST.org).

There will most likely be an advisor assigned to work with students in your major who can help you to outline your Educational Plan (sequential list of courses you will need to complete your degree or academic program). You may not be aware that they are monitoring your academic progress until you receive an email or phone call from that person asking you to come in to discuss which courses you plan to take to complete your major. Colleges and universities typically employ academic counselors that can help you to design your Educational Plan.

Don't expect your advisor to know the answer to all your questions (such as the starting salary of someone in your specific career field). Sometimes they may choose to refer you to others resources, such as the campus Career Center. There will be times when you will have to take the initiative to research information on your own. Your advisor may not have the time to research all of your questions; however, they may be able to direct you to some valuable resources to get you started on your own research.

Don't be afraid to shop around for an academic counselor or advisor. Since colleges usually employ numerous academic counselors, it may be possible to meet with different ones and then schedule return appointments with the one that is the best match for you (i.e., someone you work well with and who is a reliable source of information). When in doubt as to who you should work with, ask your fellow students- they can be very good at helping you to identify support staff and services. Once you've identified an academic advisor that works well with you, stick with them! They're more likely to remember you and the details of your educational plan than if you were to work with a different advisor each time.

TIP:

Plan on checking in with your Academic Counselor or Advisor at least once per year to make sure you are on track to meet your academic goals (e.g., graduate, transfer to a university, or apply to graduate school).

How To Work Well With Your Academic Advisor

Keep the following things in mind when meeting with your Academic Advisor:

- Don't wait until the last minute to try to schedule an appointment with an Academic Advisor. The beginning of each semester and registration periods are the worst time to try to see your Academic Advisor. Try to plan your appointment for the middle of the semester when advisors are less busy.

- Arrive on time (and even early). If you miss your appointment you may need to wait weeks for a new appointment. Advisors don't like it when you miss your appointments, so treat them like you would any other professional, and notify them well in advance if you have to reschedule your appointment. This allows them to meet with another student during that time slot.

- Take any important documents you think you may need with you to your advising session, e.g., copies of unofficial transcripts from other colleges attended, documents outlining any Advance Placement Credit you may have received in high school, and copies of Articulation Agreements you have been consulting.

- Notify the advisor if you are bound to any specific guidelines in selecting your courses by an outside agency (e.g., Veteran's Benefits, Vocational Rehabilitation, etc.). Think about what you want to ask the advisor before the session. Write out some questions in advance.

- Take a pen and paper to take notes on what the advisor tells you, or jot down notes using your cell phone. Keep your notes and any papers they give you in a folder, and bring these to future advising sessions (don't assume that you will remember all the information you were told).

- Notify the advisor of any extenuating circumstances which may affect your success in college (e.g., if you are working many hours at an outside job or have family responsibilities); the advisor may be able to refer you to additional resources, such as scholarships or child care facilities.

- Download and print any forms that you will need to complete, and take these with you to your appointment.

- Find out if there is an advisor for your specific major or for students in your department. Stop by to introduce yourself and/or to schedule an appointment with them by your second semester of college.

- Don't expect the advisor to be able to help you select classes if you have no idea what majors interest you. Try to narrow down your major interests to a couple of areas to start.

- See if there are advisors in your major or program that can answer quick questions. This can save you and the advisor from having to schedule a longer appointment. Some campuses allow you to email advisors questions related to your major.

- Look online to see if there is a "Frequently Asked Questions" section, or Guidebooks on your college website for different majors.

- Follow-up on anything your advisor asks you to do, such as filing your Graduation Petition by a certain date.

- Be sure to thank the advisor for meeting with you. Being polite ensures that they are more likely to go the extra mile to answer your future questions.

TIP:

Don't be afraid to ask questions if you're unclear about campus programs or policies. Remember, the faculty and staff are paid to assist you. Schedule appointments with key resource people to make sure you have the time to ask all your questions.

Academic Planning / Building Your Schedule

In order to earn a four year college degree in four years, you will need to take and complete approximately 15 units per semester. This plan assumes that you are not required to take any remedial courses, and that you do not have to repeat any courses. Each college major is different, and some will require numerous prerequisites or pre-major courses before you can officially enroll in your major courses. If you are completing a double major, or a major with several concentrations (e.g., a degree in Business Administration with concentrations in Finance, Marketing, and International Business) you may need to build additional semesters into your Educational Plan. If you are working at an outside job, you will want to adjust the number of units you take accordingly. Full-time students (those enrolled in 12-15 units or more) would benefit by limiting the number of hours they work to no more than 15 per week. Part-time students can work more hours; however, this may increase the number of years it takes them to complete their degree.

When planning your class schedule each semester, be sure to balance some of your more difficult courses with some that aren't as demanding. For example, don't sign up for Advanced Calculus, Chemistry, Physics, Anatomy & Physiology and The Complete Works of Shakespeare all during the same semester. Try to balance heavy reading courses or courses requiring long term papers, with others that have less reading and writing. The same goes for math or science classes; balance these with other non-math/science classes so you don't burn out from studying too much of the same material at once. You are more likely to enjoy a subject if you aren't inundated with it 24 hours a day.

Make sure that you find out about which courses you must take sequentially (i.e., you can't enroll in a particular class until you have completed a prerequisite course). Build these requirements into your long term Educational Plan, otherwise you may find that you are done with all of your required courses, except for 3 or 4 that run in sequence (which translates into 3 – 4 additional semesters in which you will have to enroll).

Consult your college catalog for official information on major and graduation requirements. Always read the fine print. If you have a hard copy of your college catalog, hold onto it, even after you graduate. You'll be surprised how years later you may want to look up the description of a course you took for employment or graduate study purposes. If you are given permission to substitute a course in your major, make sure you get this in writing from someone who is authorized to make that decision.

Remember that there are petition processes for just about everything at the college level. You can sometimes appeal a decision made by a faculty member or a policy related to your major, particularly if you have extenuating circumstances such as a serious illness. A college dean or administrator may have the authority to take extenuating circumstances into consideration that a front-line staff person might not have.

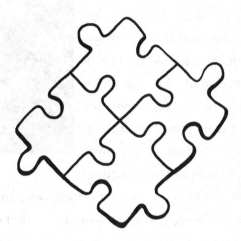

The Puzzle Analogy

Figuring out your educational/career path is a lot like trying to solve a puzzle. You're likely to interact with numerous counselors or advisors. Each person can help you to solve a piece of the puzzle. Students often make the mistake of assuming that an advisor from one college will know everything about the programs and policies of another college. Make sure that you are asking the right people for the right type of information. Don't expect a transfer counselor from the local state college to know about majors offered at local private colleges. Similarly, a university career counselor may be an excellent resource for current salary information, but won't necessarily know the graduation requirements pertaining to your degree. Don't rely on friends or classmates to provide you with accurate information about your degree requirements; while they may mean well, relying on informal sources of information may mean you end up taking unnecessary classes or missing out on needed courses. When in doubt, ask for information about campus policies and requirements in writing.

TIP:

Make the most of your summer breaks by enrolling in summer session classes, completing an internship for academic credit and/or pay, and working at an outside job and saving money so that you don't have to work so many hours at a job during the school year.

FAQ: Do I have to attend class from 9 – 5?

One of the nice things about college is that you can often set-up your schedule around your preferred study hours. So if you like to study late at night and sleep in mornings, you may be able to register for afternoon classes that allow you to do this. In college you can sometimes set up your schedule to attend classes Monday/Wednesday/Friday, or Tuesday/Thursday only. You may be able to take evening classes in order to build your class schedule around a job. The combinations of part-time or full-time work and study schedules are endless- you're bound to find something that works for you. I once met a student who took one class a semester for 17 years while she raised her children, and she eventually ended up completing a Bachelor's Degree!

Community colleges typically offer flexible course schedules. Many universities are offering more evening, weekend, and online courses to cater to working adults. Some private colleges offer classes that last only one month; the students take once class at a time, and generally meet during the evening and/or weekends. The tuition for these courses can be high, so you may have to pay for the increased flexibility in scheduling your courses. This increased cost may be worth it if this option allows you to hold on to a day job while attending classes, or if you are already working full-time but want to earn an undergraduate or graduate degree to advance in your career field.

It is important to remember that while colleges and universities try to be flexible in regards to course schedules, you may get to the point in your academic career where you have to switch gears and plan your work schedule around course offerings. This is especially true the closer you get to graduation (i.e., you may need specific courses that are offered at limited or "inconvenient" times to finish your academic program).

Have A Back-up Plan (Plan B)

When planning your course schedule for each semester (list of classes you're going to take) always map out a Plan A and a Plan B! Oftentimes students select a group of classes assuming they will have no trouble registering for them. However, many factors can affect whether or not you get your first choice of classes, or whether you get them on the days or at the times you want them. Some colleges give students who have reached senior status a higher priority for registering for classes, because they have less time to complete their degree than students who are just starting out. Some colleges will use a lottery system to assign registration priority to students. Make sure you learn early on how your college assigns priority for registering for classes, and always register for classes as soon as you are allowed each semester (before those precious class sections get filled up). If all goes well, you'll get the classes you need in a timely fashion. Sooner or later, however, you may find that the only available slots left are on Friday evenings (or some other time you'd prefer not to be in class). Don't be surprised if at some point in your college career you need to adjust your preferred schedule because of the unavailability of courses. Always be prepared with a Plan B (and even a Plan C) should you not get the courses or ideal schedule of classes you want.

When it comes to designing your Educational Plan, have a Plan A, Plan B *and* a Plan C. Update and/or revise your Educational Plan at least once per year by consulting with your Academic Counselor or Advisor. Take into consideration the progress you made the previous semesters or quarters. Should you have to repeat a class, you may want to make up those units by enrolling in a special Winter Break Session or in Summer Session. Remember that not all classes are offered each semester or quarter, so be sure to consult Class Schedules or the College Catalog, or check with the relevant department to find out when (and how often) the classes you need are offered.

- **Plan A** represents the order of your classes if all goes well (i.e., you get the classes you need when you want them, and you pass them without any problems).

- **Plan B** should outline your second choice of classes, in case you have difficulty enrolling in required courses in a timely manner.

- **Plan C** represents your desired plan of action should you have to repeat any courses or experience any serious delays getting into the courses you need. Unfortunately, with colleges and universities becoming more crowded due to record applicants and budget cuts, this is becoming more common.

PLAN A Fall Semester			
Name of Class	*Units / Credits*	*Days*	*Time*
Psych 1	3	Mon / Weds	9:00 – 10:30
Political Science	3	Mon / Weds	11:00 – 12:30
Biology	4	Tues / Thurs	1:00 – 3:00
Biology Lab	1	Tues / Thurs	3:00 – 4:30
English Composition	3	Tues / Thurs	6:00 – 7:30

PLAN B Fall Semester			
Name of Class	*Units / Credits*	*Days*	*Time*
Anthropology	3	Mon / Weds	9:00 – 10:30
Spanish 1	3	Mon / Weds	11:00 – 12:30
Chemistry	4	Tues / Thurs	12:00 – 2:00
Chemistry Lab	1	Tues / Thurs	2:00 – 3:30
Statistics	4	Tues / Thurs	5:00 – 7:00

Case Study: A Way Out

Michelle was in her senior year in high school when she found out she was pregnant. She immediately knew that her boyfriend would not want to settle down and be a father or husband. She decided that with or without her boyfriend's support, she would have her baby. Several of her cousins had had children when they were young. She saw them struggle, but they had somehow managed to survive. She knew her parents would be upset, but she believed that after their emotions subsided, they would try to help her out. Michelle's father worked long shifts at a local warehouse. Her mother worked the graveyard shift at a cannery and slept during the day. Both her parents worked lots of overtime hours to keep food on the table for Michelle and her siblings. As expected, Michelle's announcement drew mixed looks of sadness and anger from her parents. Still, they did not seem as surprised as Michelle had imagined. Lots of young women in their neighborhood were having babies. Some even joked about how they didn't have to work and still were able to buy food and clothes for their kids. They frequently lived with extended family members, and some moved in with their boyfriend or got married. Some lived in housing subsidized by the government and continued to have children even though they knew the time would come when their government benefits would end.

Michelle managed to finish high school. By the time her son Carlos was born, her boyfriend was long gone. She relied on government assistance and her parents to get her through the first year of taking care of her son, and continued to live at home with her family. Michelle had always dreamed of being an accountant. She loved taking business classes in high school; she managed her parents' finances, and had helped her aunt and uncle with the bookkeeping for their small restaurant. One day Michelle heard about a program at the local community college that was established to help single moms return to school. She found out she could place Carlos in the college's Childcare Center while she took classes, but only if she attended school full-time and worked part-time on campus. She called her cousin to see if she could watch Carlos for a while so she could attend an information meeting on campus to learn about the program to help single moms go back to school. "Why are you going to go to school when you don't have to?" her cousin answered. "Look at me. I've got it good. I don't have to pay for food or medical insurance, and my kids go to a free preschool. Why don't you just stay home and send Carlos to the preschool where my kids go?" "I just want something better for us, that's all," Michelle responded. Her cousin agreed to watch Carlos, but Michelle had a feeling that would be the last time her cousin would do her a favor. She couldn't tell if her cousin was angry or jealous at the idea of Michelle wanting to go back to school.

The night of the information session Michelle walked into a large room with about 30 other women. Some looked tired and worn out, while others talked excitedly with one another. Since she didn't know anyone else, she sat in the back of the room. The information session was led by a young woman named Monica. She introduced herself as a Peer Advisor that worked for the college. "Three years ago I was sitting where you are sitting," Monica announced. "I had two kids and was working cleaning houses to support them. I felt like I had no future for myself, and that I'd never be able to provide a good life for my kids. This semester I will finish a two year degree in Business. I work on campus in the Business Office, and our Co-op Program helped me to find an internship in an office 5 miles from where I live. If I do well in my internship, and I finish my two year degree, the owner has promised to give me a full-time job when I graduate." The rest of the session was a blur of information about how to enroll at the college and complete the forms to apply to the program. When the session ended, Michelle nervously approached Monica, and said, "Could I ask you a few questions?" "Sure," Monica responded. "What do you want to know?"

1) What do you think was the first question Michelle asked Monica?

2) Do you think it is possible to successfully attend college if you have children?

3) What advice would you give to a single parent who wants to attend college?

4) What are some things Michelle should consider and plan for during her first semester at college?

5) Who do you think would be in the best position to encourage and support Michelle while she is enrolled in college?

TIP: Take a few minutes each evening or morning to organize yourself. Make sure your TO DO LIST is up to date. Use a small notebook, or a calendar on your computer, or an app on your phone to help you keep track of the deadlines of major assignments and upcoming exams.

Things You Should Find Out/Review Prior To The Start Of Each Semester

Much of the following information can be found on your college's website or Catalog. If you have questions about services or resources that aren't listed on your college website or in the College Catalog, check to see if there is a number you can call for general information. While the person assisting you may not know the answer to all your questions, they can likely refer you to the appropriate office or resource person for more information.

- The deadline to register for classes, and to add/drop classes

- The deadline to pay tuition and fees, and to apply for refunds

- The deadline to apply for campus housing

- Where to obtain and/or update your Student ID Card, and whether you are eligible for free or reduced fees for public transportation with your Student ID Card

- The location of any services on campus you may need, including Tutoring, Academic Advising, Health Services, Counseling Services, and/or support services for students with disabilities

- The deadline to apply for financial aid (including campus-based scholarships)

- The total number of hours you will attend class each week (as well as the number of hours you will need to study for each class)

- If there is an Academic Advisor in your department that will be monitoring your progress (as well as whether that advisor can help you plan the sequence of courses you will take to complete your major requirements and degree)

- The policy on attending or missing the first class (some professors may drop you from their class if you miss the 1st session)

- Become familiar with your College Catalog, either a hard copy or the online version (this is your "contract" with the university regarding Graduation and Major Requirements)

Self-Assessment

Rate yourself on the behaviors of successful students on a scale of 1 – 5. How well prepared are you in the following areas?

    1 = I need lots of help with this

    2 = I could do better in this area

    3 = I'm OK in this area

    4 = I do a good job in this area

    5 = I'm very good at this

ORGANIZATIONAL SKILLS

____ I attend required New Student Orientation programs and advising sessions to understand how to plan my courses

____ I have a set place to keep my paperwork related to school organized

____ I have access to a computer and printer to do my homework assignments

____ I know when I am supposed to register for classes each term, and I register for classes as soon as I am able

____ I meet at least once a year with an Academic Counselor to plan and monitor my coursework and the progress towards my degree

____ I know how to access information through my college's website

____ I know exactly which courses I need to take to reach my academic goal

____ I purchase the supplies I will need prior to the start of each semester

____ I understand how to read the College Catalog and Class Schedules

____ I understand the terminology I will need to know to function in a college setting

____ I know where to go on campus to get my questions answered about different areas such as Financial Aid, Major Requirements, and Graduation Requirements

Place a checkmark next to any items that you rated a 1 (I need lots of help with this) or a 2 (I could do better in this area). Identify where you could go on campus in order to solicit help and learn more about these areas.

The following resources can help you to learn more about how to become better organized in college.

- Participating in New Student Orientation Programs and advising sessions specific to your major can help you to better understand the requirements of your degree.

- Your Academic Advisor can also answer questions about the courses you will need to take, Major Requirements, and Graduation Requirements.

- Your College Catalog will have information on annual timelines for registering for classes, as well as definitions for the new terminology you will hear frequently in college.

- Your college website will have information about Financial Aid and upcoming deadlines.

- The staff at your college bookstore can help you to determine which supplies you will need to set up a personal work station and home computer station.

- If you do not own a computer or printer, become familiar with the various computer labs available to students at your campus. Know their hours of operation and make it a point to work there during non-peak hours. Be sure to have a copy and print card loaded and available to pay for photocopying or printing.

Chapter Notes:

Things to think about...

Things to remember...

Things to do....

Chapter 4

Things That Throw Off Your Game (Barriers To Academic Success)

"I've always found that anything worth achieving will always have obstacles in the way and you've got to have that drive and determination to overcome those obstacles on route to whatever it is that you want to accomplish."

Chuck Norris

Myth #5: Most students enter college completely prepared to succeed.

If you look at the group of freshmen enrolling at your campus, you'll find that many are well-prepared for college work. However there may also be many entering students who are not ready to do college-level work, as evidenced by their scores on English and math placement tests, or by the fact that they find assignments such as writing research papers extremely challenging. This is more common in open access institutions, such as community colleges; yet, even freshmen enrolling at four year universities can struggle with college level work. It is common for students who just graduated from high school to score lower on the Math and English Assessments (tests they are required to take prior to registering for their first semester of classes) than they thought they would. I saw many examples of this when I was advising new students. They would say "I don't understand why I have to take something lower than Freshman Composition- I earned all A's in English in high school!" Just because students are good at some subjects doesn't mean they're good at all subjects. Some new students may excel at math, but have difficulty with writing courses. Some may be able to read lengthy textbooks with no problem, but struggle at giving presentations.

If you find that you enter college needing to play catch-up academically, here are few suggestions for how to do so. First, it is important that you understand your college or university's policies on completing pre-college level work. While a community college may allow you several semesters to take review or remedial courses to prepare you for college level English or math, four year colleges or universities may only allow you one year to complete any review courses you need. If at the end of that time you are not performing at the college level, they may ask you to enroll at your local community college to take additional courses in these areas before returning to the university. In order to succeed in introductory courses or upper division courses in General Education or your major, it is critical that you be able to read lengthy textbooks and write at the college level for papers and exams. Luckily, if you need assistance in these areas, there are classes available to help you to build up your math, English and computer skills. However, keep in mind that the units earned in these courses most likely will not count towards your degree. Spending time completing remedial classes may also count against any financial aid you receive (i.e., if you have to take numerous remedial classes, you may find that you run out of certain grants before you graduate). Also, the more remedial classes you have to take, the longer it will take you to complete your two or four year degree. You can see why it makes sense to do your very best in high school so that you enter college with strong math and English skills. It is also important to take the Assessment or English and Math Placement Tests seriously so that you aren't placed in courses that are too easy for you. Many colleges offer "summer bridge programs" that help students who are struggling in one or more academic areas to review needed material prior to their first semester.

TO DO:

If you need to brush up on your writing, math or computer skills prior to the start of classes, ask you Academic Advisor or admissions representative if your campus offers any pre-enrollment or summer programs you can complete.

**KEY CONCEPT: Don't go it alone! Colleges have
many support services to ensure your success.**

Myth #6: If you need to ask for help in college, you probably shouldn't be there in the first place.

When I was in college, one of the last things I wanted to do was admit that I needed help in my classes. I understand how hard it can be for college students to ask for help. What I didn't realize at the time was that successful students know *when* to ask for help. I now tell students not to be embarrassed to admit that they need tutoring in a subject. Asking for help is one of the smartest things you can do. Again, most students do not excel in all subjects- each most likely has strengths, yet may need some support in one or more areas. Studying with other students in small study groups or "Supplemental Instruction" groups can also help you to learn difficult material. In reality, students who study in groups are much more likely to be successful academically than students who study alone. Become familiar with the Tutoring Center or any tutorial labs at your campus that provide free or reduced fee individual or group tutoring to students. This can save you a large amount of money, as the cost of hiring a private tutor can be quite high. If you think that you may need some support in any of your classes, join a study group; if one doesn't exist for your class, organize one. Chances are there are other students in your class who could also use some extra help and would be willing to work in a group to better learn the material.

KEY CONCEPT: Consistency pays off. Returning each semester = degrees and increased career opportunities!

Time Management

Knowing how to manage your time is a skill that is critical to your academic success. College students generally have *very* busy schedules. Besides attending classes and keeping up with reading your textbooks, you must also complete homework assignments, write essays and research papers, and study for tests. College campuses offer lots of opportunities to get sidetracked. While attending student club meetings, campus theatrical and musical productions, or athletic events is an important part of your college experience, you have to be careful not to spend so much time in extracurricular activities that you neglect your studies. Adding to your daily "To Do" list are phone calls and texts from assorted friends and family members asking for favors or just wanting to touch base with you. Now is a good time to add the following word (gently, but firmly) to your vocabulary – "No!" While it may seem difficult at first to turn down invitations to social events or requests that are not a high priority, the more you practice the easier it will be to turn down invitations or requests that you know you simply do not have the time to participate in or fulfill.

TIP:

Really think about how much you can handle at once. If you are taking 2, 3, or 4 classes *and* working at an outside job, something usually has to give- your grades, your health, or your work performance on the job. Learn from your experience from previous semesters. If working 20 hours per week while being enrolled fulltime in college was way too much to do last semester, make sure you change something next semester- either the number of classes or units you take, or the number of hours you work at an outside job.

Time Management: Prioritization Exercise

Read through the following list of different "demands on your time" and determine the order in which you would respond to them (# 1 - #15). Pretend all these demands are occurring simultaneously. Write #1 next to the item you would attend to first, #2 next to the item you would attend to second, etc.

A)   You are supposed to turn in your Learning Styles homework packet tonight for your College Success class. You need about ½ hour to finish it.

B)   Your cellphone rings- you are being asked to participate in a survey about the upcoming election. ("It will only take a few minutes of your time.")

C)   Your mom just texted you. She hasn't heard from you in so long that your family is thinking of visiting you this weekend.

D)   Your good friend asked you to help him narrow down the list of topics for his research paper (he helped you to study for your math exam last week).

E)   Someone you met in passing at the coffee shop keeps texting you and asking "When are you going to go out with me?!!!"

F)   Your neighbor telephones. Her daughter is running a fever and she wants to take her to the doctor. She asks you to watch her son while she's gone.

G)   You have two chapters of American History to read for tomorrow's class. (You really need to pass this class in order to start your upper division courses. Also, the instructor likes to give pop quizzes "Just to see who really does their homework!")

H)   The dishwasher is making funny noises. Something's oozing out from the bottom of it...

I)   It's almost lunchtime. Your stomach is growling and you're feeling lightheaded because you skipped breakfast.

J) The receptionist at the dentist's office calls you. A space just opened up for a 3:30 cleaning. You've been trying to get an appointment for months.

K) Your teenage cousin has the TV on so loud you can't think clearly.

L) You don't have any clean clothes to wear to school tonight.

M) You could really use a nap. (You feel a cold coming on.)

N) Your supervisor calls. She wants to know if you can work overtime this week, as several of your coworkers have called in sick. She'll pay you double your regular hourly wage, but you have to commit right now to working the extra hours.

O) That special someone just called and asked you to go out to dinner tonight.

Answer the following questions:

Which item did you rank as number one?

Why would you respond to that demand on your time first over the others?

Which did you rank number 2?

Why was that the second most important item for you?

Which items did you rank the lowest?

Why would you respond to these time demands last?

Time Management Challenges Of Different Groups

Take a few minutes to brainstorm the typical and unique time management challenges of each of the following groups of students:

Freshmen living at home and working at an outside job (e.g., requests to attend family events)

Freshman living in the dorms (e.g., roommates who have lots of visitors)

Students with children (e.g., no quiet time to study)

List two possible solutions to address each typical time management problem.

Freshmen living at home and working at an outside job (e.g., block out time on your weekly calendar for studying and tell others that you already have a commitment you can't cancel)

Freshman living in the dorms (e.g., ask your roommate to agree to certain hours where no visitors will be in the room so you know you can study, or go to the Library to study).

Students with children (e.g., study after the kids are in bed for the night)

Which of these groups of students can you relate to the most?

How have you handled problems in the area of your own time management?

Journal Assignment:

Spend 15 minutes writing about how you can make the best use of your time in college.

FAQ: What's the difference between the Semester and the Quarter System?

The majority of colleges and universities operate on the semester system. Students enroll in classes that last 16 – 18 weeks each Fall and Spring Semester. Students on the semester system sometimes have the option to enroll in classes during a short winter intersession between Fall and Spring Semesters. Taking courses during summer session is also a way for students to take courses and reduce the number of years it takes to complete a degree.

Some colleges operate on the Quarter system; students enroll in 10 - 12 week Fall, Winter, and Spring sessions, or quarters. Taking classes in the summer is also an option for these students. Either way, a four year degree shouldn't take any longer to complete through the Semester System than through the Quarter System. While the unit calculation is different in the two systems, the overall length of time spent in college to earn any specific degree is the same.

When applying to colleges, or preparing to transfer from a community college to a four year university, you may want to consider whether you prefer the Semester or Quarter System. The semester system is preferable for students who want to take their time studying a subject and absorbing the learning material. Some students find it difficult to maintain interest in required courses when they stretch over 16-18 weeks. For students who prefer a quicker pace, the Quarter System may be ideal. However, one of the disadvantages of the Quarter System is that midterm and final exams occur earlier. This can be challenging for students who want or need more prep time.

If you attend a college or university that operates on the Quarter System, you will find that each term starts and ends quickly. This can be both interesting and challenging. In order to make the Quarter System work for you, keep in mind the following suggestions:

- Plan for earlier mid-term exams and finals. Note important deadlines on your calendar at the start of the quarter.

- With potentially fewer class sessions required, regular attendance is key to maintaining good grades. Missing a class session means missing more material than if you were attending classes in the Semester System.

- Keep up with the required textbook readings. If possible, purchase your textbooks prior to the start of each quarter and begin to review then during any breaks before the next quarter starts.

Case Study: The Study Group

Raquel and Jesse dated each other exclusively their last two years of high school. After high school Jesse immediately enrolled in a technical training program through a private school, and Raquel registered to take Fall Semester classes at a community college to become a registered nurse. Things seemed fine between them the summer after high school. Jesse started his technical program and Raquel worked part-time at the mall. They saw each other often. Jesse was looking forward to completing his 12 month technical training so that he and Raquel could get married. However, things seemed to change when Raquel started her classes. She was still working part-time, and she was taking a full load of nursing prerequisites. She hadn't imagined that she would need to study so much to keep up in her classes. Luckily, she had a group of classmates she studied with to prepare for upcoming exams.

Jesse became increasingly frustrated that Raquel was not available to go out with him as frequently because of her school load and her job. At first he would leave messages on her cell phone teasing her about how she spent more time with her books than with him. Then he began to inquire about who was in her study group. Were there any guys studying to be nurses? "Actually," she responded, "there are two guys in our study group and four women." Once he found out that Raquel was spending several hours each week with her study partners, he became more irritable. "Just exactly what are you studying?" he demanded, when she told him she couldn't meet him because she had an upcoming test in Anatomy. He then began texting her from his classes several times a day, insisting that she report in with him on what she was doing. Sometimes she was afraid to answer the phone when he called because she could never tell when he was going to be in a bad mood.

Raquel loved her new major. She was doing well in her classes and knew that she had what it takes to become a registered nurse. In fact, she was doing so well, one of her nursing instructors asked her if she had ever considered becoming a nurse practitioner or a physician's assistant. The instructor told her about a program at a local university that offered a Master's degree that would allow her to work in the health field and be paid more than a registered nurse. One night, Jesse showed up at her house and insisted that she go for a car ride with him. She could tell he was angry. He had been angry a lot lately. He began to raise his voice and tell her that he was fed up with her schedule, and that she never had any time for him. He told her he would be done soon with his technical degree and was sure to get a good job that could support both of them. He told her "You won't have to work. You can stay home and take care of our kids when we have them." She was sure Jesse was going to break up with her right then and there, but was shocked when Jesse handed her a small box with a ribbon. Inside was an engagement ring. "I want us to set our wedding date for this summer," he told her. Raquel sat there, staring at the ring, and wondered what to do next.

1) What goals does Jesse have for his life?

2) What goals does Raquel have for her life?

3) If you were friends with Raquel, what advice would you give her?

4) If you were friends with Jesse, what advice would you give him?

5) Have you ever been in a situation where you faced conflicting goals? How did you resolve the situation?

Dealing With Setbacks

There's a saying that goes "Take two steps forward, one step backward." Just when you think you're progressing in life, you may encounter a setback, albeit a minor one. You may be making good progress towards earning a college degree, when you unexpectedly flunk a required course and have to repeat it. Or, you might be on-course career-wise, and the job market changes, forcing you to take a cut in pay or to find a new job. While temporary setbacks might make you feel like dropping out of college or switching careers, it's important to stay focused on your long term goals in order to continue moving forward. Knowing what you want in the future related to your education and career, and other major areas of your life, can keep you from being overwhelmed by minor setbacks.

For example, if you encounter difficulty in a math or writing course, you may think about changing your major, or even whether you should try to earn a degree. However, if you see the course in perspective (e.g., you understand that you only need to complete one or two courses in this area to earn your degree) this can help you to overcome the fear that this particular problem will force you to overhaul your plans. Setting clear goals (e.g., "I want to earn a Bachelor's Degree in order to compete for higher paying jobs) can also help you to stay focused through difficult times.

Anticipating potential problems ahead of time can help you to deal with them should they occur. For example, knowing that you have difficulty with quantitative or writing courses can be the catalyst to help you identify support services, such as tutoring, in advance. Knowing that your employer plans to eliminate your department in two years is a great impetus for updating your resume, upgrading your job skills, or attending career development workshops.

Overcoming Barriers To Academic Success

In each of the following major areas of your life, identify potential setbacks you could encounter that could affect your ability to be successful in college. For each potential problem, list two things you could do to address or resolve that problem.

Sample:

Major Area: **Career**

Potential Setbacks: *I could encounter difficulty finding a job in my field*

Possible Solutions: *Gain internship experience prior to graduation*

                        Complete a double major in college so I can compete for jobs in more than one area

Major Area: **Education**

Potential Setbacks:

Possible Solutions:

Major Area: **Finances (housing, transportation, health insurance)**

Potential Setbacks:

Possible Solutions:

Major Area: **Paying for college**

Potential Setbacks:

Possible Solutions:

Major Area: **Time Management**

Potential Setbacks:

Possible Solutions:

Major Area: **Health / Wellness**

Potential Setbacks:

Possible Solutions:

Major Area: **Family**

Potential Setbacks:

Possible Solutions:

Major Area: **Relationships**

Potential Setbacks:

Possible Solutions:

Major Area: **Job**

Potential Setbacks:

Possible Solutions:

Major Area: **Career**

Potential Setbacks:

Possible Solutions:

Time Management & Schedule Building Tips

- Prior to the start of each semester, take a quick inventory of your school supplies and see what you need to purchase so you'll be ready for classes.

- Are you working lots of hours to help pay your way through college? Consider taking online or TV courses to fill out your schedule.

- Spend some time each weekend organizing your schedule for the upcoming week. Make sure the dates of assignments, quizzes and exams are posted, as well as blocks of study time you will need to excel academically.

- Don't overload yourself taking too many units or credits each term. You may end up dropping some of those classes later, which means you'll have to repeat them.

- Don't burn the candle at both ends. Make sure you get enough sleep each night so that you are awake during class and when it comes time to study.

- Take advantage of the time between classes to study, review lecture notes for your next class, visit your professors during their office hours, or participate in extracurricular activities. Those short sessions can add up to hours of extra study time each week. Always keep one of your textbooks handy (or access online or E-versions of your textbooks) so you can turn the breaks between classes or work into study sessions.

- Go to campus on days even when you do not have classes in order to meet with academic counselors, use the library, participate in study groups, or access support services such as free tutoring.

- Use the time between classes to take a brisk walk around campus. Keeping your energy level up will enable you to handle longer class sessions. Pack some snacks to carry you through the day; waiting in long cafeteria lines could cause you to be late for class.

- Look for breaks in your schedule to attend free campus workshops on topics such as Effective Note-taking, Dealing With Test Anxiety, and Career Exploration.

- Enroll in Summer Session to complete required classes. Also consider enrolling in late-start, weekend, or online courses to make the most of each semester.

- Register early for classes each semester. You'll increase the chance of getting the classes you need at the days/times you prefer.

- When creating your schedule each semester, be sure to take into consideration the amount of time it will take to get from one class to another, or to commute to and from campus.

- Have a few minutes to spare? Spend some time perusing your college's website. You'll find lots of helpful information on it, including how to access many free campus support services such as tutoring or personal counseling.

- Consider cutting back on your work hours when you have a full day of classes. Try to set-up your job schedule to work more on days you don't attend classes. Or, look for an on-campus job, then schedule your work hours during breaks between classes.

- Do you need to find out when your college or university will be closed for upcoming holidays? Check the campus website for this and other important dates, such as the deadlines for adding and dropping classes this term.

- Practice saying 'NO' ahead of time so that you really can turn down social invitations or the inevitable requests for favors you will receive throughout the semester or quarter.

TIP:

Be aware that if you miss the first class session of the semester or quarter, you may be dropped from the class. Make sure you know your campus policy regarding class attendance, as well as each instructor's attendance policy. Also, don't assume that your professor will automatically drop you if you don't show up to any classes. Many students have been surprised to receive an F grade in a course they registered for, but never attended.

Myth #7 - If you take longer than four years to complete a Bachelor's degree, you are a failure.

Many students take more than four years to complete a four year college degree. There are numerous reasons for this. Sometimes students have responsibilities such as taking care of family members, or they have to work a certain number of hours at an outside job to pay for school. These factors can affect the number of hours they have available each week to take classes and to study. Sometimes students change their major, and this can result in having to take additional classes, especially if they decide late in the game that they want to switch to a different academic area. Some students opt to do a double major, which may add extra time to their degree. Frequently, students are affected by things outside of their control. For example, at some campuses, you might find that there are so many students trying to get into classes, that you can't get the classes that you need when you want them. If you are a senior and you can't get the last classes you need, this can add an extra semester or more to your studies, which consequently delays your graduation and possibly your entrance into the workforce. Don't become dismayed if you find it takes an extra semester, or an extra year or more to complete your college degree. Be sure to work closely with academic counselors to plan your schedule each semester so that you don't waste time taking any unnecessary courses. Take advantage of summer sessions to earn needed units, and always have a Plan B (i.e., know which courses you can take if you don't get into the ones you want each semester). There is a certain amount of luck that's needed to get the classes you want when you want them. Some colleges use a lottery system when allowing students to register each semester. Some campuses give a higher registration priority for students who are in their last year of study. Always register for classes as soon as you are able (pay attention to your priority registration dates). With a little luck, and with good planning, you can avoid extending your degree longer than it should take to complete.

Self Esteem: Avoid The Trap Of Comparing Yourself To Others…

Amber had been a strong student in high school. She'd dreamed of attending a top university, even though neither of her parents had gone to college and they weren't going to be able to help her out financially. She was thrilled when she was accepted to several colleges. She opted to attend the most expensive university to which she had been accepted because they had a solid academic reputation and they offered her an excellent financial aid package.

By the start of her junior year, she had earned mostly A's and B's in her Business Major. She had a decent social life, and she was looking forward to graduating and going to work as a financial planner. Nevertheless, once in a while, Amber would mentally beat herself up over what she "hadn't accomplished" in life. She would compare herself to the other students in her dorm, and become depressed over the fact that they had nicer clothes or drove better cars than she did. Her freshman year she had obsessed about whether to join a sorority. It seemed that joining a fraternity or sorority was *the* thing to do among new students. The thought of having an immediate circle of friends to socialize with had been appealing. However, when she realized she neither had the money nor the time to participate in all the Greek activities, she decided to focus on her academics instead. Still, she felt envious watching the other students rushing the frats and sororities- they seemed to be having the time of their life.

When something good happened to Amber, she'd walk around on Cloud Nine all day. A guy she had liked for some time asked her to attend a campus dinner with him; she couldn't wait for that date. One day her Economics professor complimented her on a paper she had written. She beamed when he said, "You're one of the best writers I've had in my classes." Still, if something bad happened to her, she'd obsess about it for days. Sometimes she'd think about all the things her classmates had that she didn't; she couldn't help but feel that she would be happier if she was more like them. She made it a point to avoid constantly checking social media sites, because she didn't seem to have as many "friends" as other people she knew. Whenever she'd read an update from someone who looked like they were having a great time, she'd think how her life looked insignificant compared to theirs.

Amber held a variety of part-time jobs to help pay for her college education. She worked as a teller at a local bank, and as a waitress at a small restaurant. She earned great tips working the dinner shift and had saved enough money to buy a more reliable car. On her way to class one day, Amber ran into her former dorm roommate Debbie who was in her senior year, and was stunned to learn that she had recently completed a paid internship for a prestigious accounting firm. "They offered to hire me full-time when I graduate!" Debbie exclaimed, and then proceeded to daydream aloud about the condominium she planned to buy as soon as she graduated. "I wish I could have an internship like that," she thought as Debbie rattled off a list of other items she would buy once she started the job. For the next few days Amber dragged around campus with the thought of Debbie's smiling face in the back of her mind. It wasn't that she disliked Debbie- they'd always gotten along fine. Still, Debbie had seemed so successful and she wondered why she couldn't be more like her. Never mind the fact that she thought Accounting was boring, and that the idea of working in that field for her entire career made her cringe.

Even though at a gut level Amber knew that outward signs of material success had nothing to do with a person's worth as a human being, she still felt herself getting sucked into negative thought patterns and comparing herself to others she believed were doing better than she was in life. Her accomplishments always seemed minor compared to what they had achieved. Amber decided that she needed to talk to someone who could help her to sort out her feelings of inferiority, so she made an appointment to speak to a counselor on campus. The counselor asked her why she felt like she had to compete with others. Amber responded that she had always been a good student, but that her mother had regularly pushed her to find a career where she could make a lot of money so she could move to a better neighborhood than the one where she'd been raised. She felt a lot of responsibility to succeed to help out her family. The counselor then asked her how she felt being at a highly selective university had affected her. "Everyone's always talking about how much money they're going to make in their future careers or they're bragging about which graduate program they are going to attend. It's like one-upping each other is a daily occurrence and failure is not an option. If you say you want to work in a field where you won't make a ton of money, everyone looks down on you."

The counselor responded, "There are probably many reasons why you compare yourself to others. One may be that this *is* a very competitive environment that attracts highly motivated students. One way to deal with the pressure is to walk away from situations where others are bragging about their plans. Ignore them and tell yourself 'I choose to do what makes ME happy.' You may have to make a conscious choice to do this over and over again. Truth be told, it's hard work trying to keep up with the Jones's and, frankly, it NEVER ends. If you constantly compare yourself to others, you'll never run out of things to covet- now it's their grades and internships; later it will be their car, their house, their vacations, and their "perfect" spouse; even their children will seem more successful than yours!" She continued, "Understanding and valuing your own gifts is key to getting through those times when you feel less worthy. So is adhering to the belief that each person is infinitely valuable, no matter what degrees they earn or how much money they make. Realizing that each of us has a different 'calling' in life, something to do that is uniquely ours- a job that no one else can do, because it has our name imprinted on it- is vital. Befriending the lonely, nurturing children, developing life-saving medications, cleaning up the environment -whether it is collecting trash from your local park, or inventing new ways to reuse precious resources- all these are occupations that are vital to society in the big scheme of things. Without them, quite simply, the world just wouldn't work. Ask yourself, 'Would I really be happy living someone else's life? Would I be willing to take all that this person has experienced in order to have what looks so appealing on the surface? Would I want to trade places with this other person- switch my lot in life for theirs?'" Amber thought for a moment and responded, "Well, honestly, no. I'd be very nervous about trading places with someone else, if it meant I had to take all the bad things that happened to them along with the good." "I'm going to give you an assignment to work on before our next session," the counselor stated, "and then we'll talk about it together. I want you to spend an entire hour, without stopping, writing me a letter about your strengths and the things you are grateful for in your life. I can tell you that after counseling hundreds of students at this campus, periods where you feel inadequate in life are normal and to be expected. I want to help you to not fall victim to those thoughts. Let's work together to replace those negative thoughts with positive affirmations about what makes you unique and valuable."

Journal Assignment:

Part #1: Pretend you are Amber. Start writing the letter to the counselor. Focus on Amber's strengths and accomplishments, and elaborate on what she has to look forward to in life. Give her some suggestions on how to become more positive, and how to focus less on comparing herself to others.

Part #2: Spend some time writing about your own self esteem. What lifts it up? What brings it down? What can you do to maintain a healthy self esteem?

Self-Assessment

Rate yourself on the behaviors of successful students on a scale of 1 – 5. How well prepared are you in the following areas?

1 = I need lots of help with this

2 = I could do better in this area

3 = I'm OK in this area

4 = I do a good job in this area

5 = I'm very good at this

TIME MANAGEMENT

____   I have a set time for doing chores, e.g., helping at home with chores (if applicable), doing my laundry, cleaning my room

____   I know how to make good use of time between classes to study

____   I have a calendar that is easily available to me where I write down the dates assignments are due and note upcoming exams

____   I use an electronic calendar application that automatically sends me reminders before due dates

____   I take advantage of online classes to reach my academic goal

____   I know how to plan my class schedule each semester so I don't overload myself with too many responsibilities

____   I plan ahead to socialize with my friends instead of responding to last minute requests and invitations

____   I make sure I get enough sleep

____   I study well in advance of tests so I don't have to do last minute cramming

Place a checkmark next to any items that you rated a 1 (I need lots of help with this) or a 2 (I could do better in this area). Identify where you could go on campus in order to solicit help and learn more about these areas.

The following information can help you to learn more about how to be better organized in college.

- Before the next semester, quarter or term begins, take some time to plan out your schedule.

- Include time for tasks such as doing your laundry, commuting (or getting to and from classes), studying, reading textbooks, preparing for exams and even getting enough sleep.

- Build some fun time in when you can relax or socialize with friends. Determine how much time you have per week between classes and develop a mini study plan to fill that time.

- Work with your academic counselor so that you don't take on too many classes or commitments each semester.

- Take advantage of electronic calendars and apps that will enable you to manage your time better.

Chapter Notes:

Things to think about...

Things to remember...

Things to do....

Chapter 5

Play To Win

"Those who go to college and never get out are called professors."

Anonymous

Why You Should Be In Class:
Your Professor Called - She Can't Start Without You

Does it really matter if you show up to class when you're in college? Does anyone notice? Does anyone really care? Why should you bother to go to class, especially when your friends are all headed to lunch or off campus for some fun? Here are some compelling reasons why you *should* show up to class.

In high school your teachers probably took attendance every day. If you missed more than a couple of classes, chances are your teachers noticed. If you missed several classes during the semester, it probably counted negatively against your grade. If you were gone for an extended period of time, your parents most likely received a phone call from some school official inquiring why you haven't been showing up (especially if you're under 16 years of age). In college, all of that changes, or at least, it appears to change.

If you're taking a large lecture class in college (200 – 600 students), chances are the professor will never take attendance. So, theoretically, you could miss lots of classes and no one would notice, and it wouldn't necessarily count against your grade. You could rely on reading your textbooks to learn the material that will be on the final exam. If you could learn everything you need from your textbooks, you'd never have to go to class- right? While some individuals *are* able to miss classes and still ace the final exam, these students are few and far between. Most students really need to hear the lecture, take notes, and think about the material in numerous ways in order to learn it. They absorb the material in manageable portions over the entire semester by listening to lectures, writing down notes, reading and high-lighting their textbooks, and reviewing their notes. Frequently they will form study groups with other students in their classes, or schedule appointments with campus tutors to review difficult chapters or concepts. Faculty members draw from their lectures, textbook readings, the material presented by guest speakers, and outside sources (such as articles assigned via the Internet) to develop midterm and final exams. The day you decide to cut class to go to the coffee house with your friends may be the day that the professor mentions details that will mysteriously appear on the next quiz or test.

In smaller lecture classes, your professors may or may not keep track of attendance. Some will clearly state on their course syllabus that attendance is taken into consideration when assigning grades for the class. Others may not mention a specific attendance policy, and others will state that attendance is not part of your grade. Don't believe them! Faculty members won't necessarily tell you this, but they feel good when all of their students show up to class. This validates them as instructors. They believe that they have important information to offer you (and they do), and that you will make a better professional in your field, become a well-informed citizen, and understand their subject and the world at large better because of the time you spend with them over the semester. In smaller classes where the professor is apt to notice if you're absent, chances are he or she will remember whether you were in class or seemed to go missing frequently, when assigning grades. This is especially true when your grade borders between a B and a C, or a C and a D.

Here's a key reason you should attend class- you paid for it. Would you go to a restaurant and order an eight course meal, then willingly pay the bill if half the courses were never served? Of course not! Would you buy a pair of expensive jeans if the one of the pant legs was missing? I don't think so. So why would you pay top dollar for college classes and then essentially waste your money by not showing up? If you are using financial aid to pay for college, you might think "Well, it's not my money anyway, so it's no big deal!" Or if your parents are footing the bill, you might think "What mom and dad don't know won't hurt them—as long as I graduate that's all that matters." The bottom line is *someone* is paying for you to attend college- you, your parents, or the local taxpayers. If you're paying for your own college education, you most likely will want to get your money's worth. If your parents are paying for your education, they will definitely want to know that you have not wasted their hard-earned money. And if you are lucky enough to receive financial aid such as grants or scholarships, the taxpayers or benefactors want to know that you have made the most of the opportunity you've been given.

Let's say that you attend a private college at the cost of $50,000 per year. If you take 15 units a semester, and each unit entails one hour of lecture per week, and each semester lasts 16 weeks, then each hour of lecture is costing you approximately $104! So if you blow off classes a total of 10 times during the semester, you have essentially lost or wasted over $1000 of your education. While hanging out at the coffee house or skipping class to go to the beach with your friends might seem like fun, you should ask yourself, "Is it really worth $100 of my money (or my parents' money) for every hour of class I miss to hang out with my friends?" To get a sense for how much money $100 is, count to 100 – slowly. Then think about how many hours you have to work at an outside job to earn $100 (don't forget to include the taxes that are taken out of your paycheck). How about your parents? How many hours would they have to work to give you $100 towards school?

It's up to you to make the most of the learning opportunity college provides. And chances are, you'll learn more if you show up to class. College students are expected to be, and act like mature adults. Whereas in high school the students pretty much had to be there, whether they wanted to or not, in college the professors believe that you are there of your own free will, and that you want to be there, and they expect you to act accordingly. College is also good practice for learning how to deal with the future pressures of the work world. In college, if you miss class, the worst thing that might happen is you may flunk the class and have to retake it. However, in the world of work, if you repeatedly don't show up, you'll probably get fired. College is a great place for learning patience and how to sacrifice to achieve your long term goals.

In class, professors will likely go off on tangents aside from their lecture notes. This is where you can gain insight into the passion that the instructors feel for their subject. Sure, there are certain key points you must learn to pass the class, but what makes the material interesting? How does the material matter outside of class? What can you take from the lectures and apply in your career or in an outside setting? By attending class, you may be inspired by the lecture to delve further into the subject matter, or realize this is what you really want to major in, or find yourself bringing up what you learned at home or to classmates outside of the classroom setting because it catches your attention. Sometimes what you learn is that you are lucky you only have to take one class like this, or in this subject area, or with this specific professor, because it/he simply does not interest you. Even that is valuable learning- knowing what you don't like! You would not want to major in something that you find boring. It is better to find that out by making sure you are in class so you really understand the subject matter.

Here's another reason you should not miss class- they can't start (or learn) without you! Classrooms provide the opportunity for students to learn from each other. There is a synergistic effect to classrooms. If an instructor assigns students to work in small groups to solve a problem, the potential for success (lively discussions, effective problem solving) is exponentially greater given more participants. You may be the person in your group that will see the answer to a problem clearly- but if you're gone, the whole group may miss out. And if you miss a dynamic group discussion, you'll never be able to recapture what was shared.

What are valid reasons for not attending class? Certainly, if you are sick you should stay home or in your dorm room until you feel better and you know you're not contagious. If a relative or someone close to you passes away, you will most likely want to attend the funeral and/or need some time to grieve. You may need to miss a class due to official business for another class (e.g., attending a mandatory field trip). College professors are more than willing to work with you given extenuating circumstances. If you've had perfect attendance all semester, they're more likely to believe you when you email them at the end of the semester to notify them you're sick. Some professors will ask for a doctor's note if you're going to miss more than a couple of days. Reasons professors are likely to count absences against you include: "I couldn't get a ride to campus" (they don't want to hear your sob story), "I missed the bus" (they want you to be mature enough to work through your transportation issues on your own), "I had to take care of my little brother/little sister/ailing relative/ friend who was having a crisis" (they don't care about your personal life), or, "I went to hear a speaker visiting campus from another department" (they want to be more important to you than the million distractions found around campus).

If these reasons for attending class don't convince you of the importance of showing up, remember that today's classmates may be tomorrow's professional contacts. You just may end up working for, or with, one or more of your classmates. Critical professional networking takes place in college classrooms, albeit, informally. Your professors may also be the ones you turn to for graduate school or employment recommendations. If you attended class, faithfully, those letters are much more likely to be glowing than if you weren't in class because you were hanging out with your friends.

Journal Assignment:

How many times do you typically miss class per semester?

What do you consider a good reason for missing class?

What's the worst/silliest reason you have heard of for someone missing class?

How would you handle another student in your study group or project team who repeatedly misses class or sessions, especially if your group will be assigned one grade based on everyone's input?

Things You Should Find Out About Your Major

- Who is the department advisor for students in your major (and where is their office located)?

- The number of required units/courses for your major

- The minimum GPA required for courses in your major

- Any prerequisite courses required to enter the major

- Whether there is a limit on the number of times you can take or attempt to take a course

- Whether courses in your major can also count towards General Education requirements

KEY CONCEPT: The behaviors of success college students can be learned.

TIP:

Take some time to get to know your professors. Meet with them during their office hours and ask them for career advice. When it comes time to apply for scholarships, to graduate school or for employment, you'll be able to call on them for assistance.

What You Should Know About Your Professors

The Good News:

Most professors love to work with students and love to teach- that's why they chose a career in education. Don't be afraid to approach them (they are getting paid to work with you).

Professors generally care about you, and your success in their class and in your future career. They are often willing to serve as formal and informal advisors, and can write letters of support for you if you apply to graduate school or for a job.

Professors have "office hours" assigned for each class. They are available to meet with you to answer questions or to clarify concepts they brought up in class. Professors want you to visit them during their office hours.

Many professors will take the time to get to know their students by name. To facilitate this happening, visit your professors during their office hours. This can help immensely should you need to ask them for a letter of recommendation later in your college career.

Some professors are willing to work with students outside of class (for example, serve as advisors to student clubs). If you're in a campus organization, or you're starting a new campus club, you might consider asking one of your instructors to serve as the club advisor (especially if you know the club focuses on an area in which they're also interested).

Some professors are so good at teaching their subject, they will make you want to change your major to their discipline.

Professors are human. If you take the time to get to know them, you'll find they have families, hobbies, shop at the local grocery store, and are concerned about many of the things that concern you.

Interesting Stuff:

Professors like it when you take more than one class from them, especially if you are good student.

If you ask other students, they will tell you who they think are good professors. They will also tell you which professors to avoid.

Professors know which of their colleagues have a good reputation as teachers. They also know some professors have not so great reputations.

All professors have a supervisor or boss over them, usually a "Dean." If you have a serious complaint or concern about a professor (such as the professor consistently cancels class meetings, or s/he does not follow and honor their syllabus) you can report it to the Dean.

Some of your professors struggled academically. Your math professor may have struggled to pass English, and your English professor may have struggled to pass Math. Some professors can be empathetic with students who are struggling with academic material.

Some professors are uncomfortable dealing with students on a personal level. They are more comfortable talking to students from behind a podium.

Some professors are so worried about getting tenure that they focus on that (and not on you and your class). This may mean they are hard to get a hold of outside of class.

Caution:

Most Deans were professors in their former life. They should listen to you if you have a complaint about a professor. If you feel a complaint you have brought to a Dean is not taken seriously, you can usually appeal your case or take the issue to the Dean's supervisor (usually a Vice President of Instruction).

Your professors notice if you miss class- especially if the class is small. They may hold absences against you when it comes to assigning grades (even if they said attendance does not count towards your grade).

Some professors act as if their class is the only one in which you are enrolled. They aren't aware or worried that you have three research papers all due at the same time this semester.

Some professors are never around for their office hours. If this is the case, see if any Teaching Assistants (graduate students assigned to your class) are available to help you with your questions.

Not all of your professors had teaching as their first choice for a career. Some are teaching because their first career choice or occupation didn't materialize. Some of your professors wish they could be somewhere else.

Most professors have a Master's degree or Doctorate in their subject matter. Unfortunately, many professors have never taken a class on how to teach. Some think teaching consists of lecturing for hours on end. Some professors don't know how to use or aren't comfortable with other teaching tools- so they lecture, and lecture, and lecture... If you prefer more hand-on learning, ask your classmates which professors they would recommend.

If you consistently arrive late, walk out of class to take cell phone calls, surf the web during class, or send text messages, your professors will not be happy, and they will remember this when assigning grades.

Professors want you to come to class prepared. Never ask the professor for pencils, paper, or other supplies.

If professors are "tenured," it can be very difficult for them to be fired.

Some professors derive ego fulfillment from having advanced degrees and instructing others. This comes across in the way they address students. Some professors will even brag about their courses being difficult. If you ask your classmates, they are usually willing to share with you which professors you should avoid.

A few professors have no sympathy for students that struggle in their classes. If you can't cut the mustard, they want you to drop their class. Some may actually think that certain groups (e.g., women) don't belong in their classes or discipline.

"What I Wish I'd Known In College"

On your quest to become a successful college student, don't reinvent the wheel. Seek out mentors or role models who can give you valuable advice on what it takes to succeed in college.

Interview someone who previously attended college; select someone who completed their academic goal, and who either had the same major as you, or is working in the career field you plan to enter. Answer the following questions:

Name:

Number of years they attended college:

Certificates and/or degrees earned:

Current occupation:

1)   On a scale of 1 – 10 *(1 = terrible and 10 = outstanding)*, how would you rate your overall college experience?

2)   What was the best part of college for you?

3)   Why did you select your particular major?

        Did you ever change your major?

4)   Were there any courses where you needed extra assistance?

        If yes, which ones?

        Did you seek tutorial assistance for these courses?

5) Were you involved in any extracurricular activities while you were in college, such as pre-professional clubs, community service, or student government? If so, which ones?

6) How long did it take you to complete your degree or program?

Did it take you longer to complete your degree or program than you originally expected?

7) Did you complete any job-related internships in college?

If yes, what did you learn during the internship that has helped you in your career?

If no, do you think that completing a college internship would have been helpful to you (now that you've been working in your career area for a while)?

8) What were some obstacles you had to overcome in order to complete your academic goal and/or enter your career field?

How did you overcome these obstacles?

9)   Did you have any mentors while you were in college or when you first entered your career field?

        If yes, how did you go about identifying your mentors (through a formal campus program, through social or community organizations, etc.)?

10)   What are some courses you did not take in college that you wish you had taken?

11)   Do you feel you were prepared for college (academically)?

        If yes, what helped you to be prepared?

        If no, what skills were you missing when you started college?

12)   How did you finance your education (jobs, student loans, scholarships)?

13)   What do you know now that you wish you had known in college (that would have helped you in college)?

14) Based on your overall college experience, what advice would you give to new college freshman to help them achieve academic and career success?

15) Have you been able to contribute to your work setting because of the major you studied?

16) Looking back, would you choose a different college major in order to be better-prepared in your field/job?

If yes, which major would you select & why?

If no, why not?

Case Study: Uninformed

Ryan knew he needed to do something after high school, so he decided to enroll at the local community college. He ignored the letter announcing the New Student Orientation session so he could go with a group of high school friends to the beach for a week for one last bash before college started. Not knowing how to pick his classes, he flipped through the Class Schedule and chose 4 classes that looked interesting and seemed related to the major he wanted to study- Criminal Justice. "Seventeen units sounds good," he thought. "This is way better than high school. I only have to be in class 17 hours per week, so I can work half-time and fix-up my truck." The second week of classes, Ryan's boss called him and offered him an Assistant Manager's position. He would get a $2.00 an hour raise, but would have to commit to 30 hours of work per week. "Great," Ryan thought, "Now I can really fix up my truck the way I want." At first, Ryan appears to do OK; he spends 17 hours per week in class, and works 30 hours per week. His boss is really happy with his work performance. When he logs onto the Internet to check his midterm grades, Ryan realizes he is pulling a C in one class and D's in the others. Frustrated, he goes to his room and sees that his credit card bill has just arrived. He owes $4000 including the amount he spent on new tires and rims for his truck last month.

1)   What is the biggest problem Ryan is facing?

2)   What are other problems Ryan must resolve?

3)   If Ryan were to start the school year over again, what are some mistakes he should avoid?

4)   How could Ryan improve his situation?

5)   If Ryan does not change his behavior, what is likely to happen to him in the future?

Chapter Notes:

Things to think about...

Things to remember...

Things to do....

Chapter 6

You've Got To Pay To Play
(Financing Your Education)

*Bumper sticker: "Driver carries no cash- he has
a son in college."*

Anonymous

Money Management

Wouldn't it be great if college was free?! Think of all the headaches you could avoid when it comes time to paying for tuition and books. However, unless your parents are fabulously wealthy, you have recently won the lottery, or you have been awarded a full scholarship, you will inevitably have to figure out how you will cover your college expenses. Even if you have enough money to pay all your bills, you must still meet deadlines for payments and track your expenses to make sure you don't overspend your budget. As with other things, practice makes perfect. Instead of just spending freely, keep track of your expenses each month and give yourself a weekly budget. If you know you have $30 to spend on luxuries each week, you can buy that café mocha or go out for pizza with your friends without worrying that it will break the bank later.

Paying for college can be challenging for some students. The high cost of textbooks, dorm fees, meal plans and social outings may make you wonder how you will pay for it all without going into massive debt. Developing an annual budget and breaking it down by semester or quarter will also help ensure that you don't run out of funds at an inopportune time. In order to know how much money you will need per year, you must have a clear understanding of all your expenses, including everything from tuition and parking fees, to snacks and weekend movie tickets. You will want to list all sources of income, from summer job earnings and school-year jobs or internships, to cash gifts from parents, and money you can borrow in the form of student loans. Should you find that your expenses outweigh your income, you will either have to come up with new ways to generate money (e.g., selling back your textbooks to the campus bookstore at the end of each term or finding a part time job), or you'll have to figure out how to cut back on your expenses. You can also meet expenses by simultaneously cutting your expenditures and increasing your income. Check your college or university Career Center to see if they have a jobs board or a website where they advertise short term jobs, such as house sitting or seasonal positions during the holidays. Short term jobs can help you to raise needed cash quickly without committing to a regular or permanent job.

Myth #8 - College is too expensive for most people to attend.

It's true that college can be very expensive. However, don't let that keep you from pursuing or completing a college degree, as you may be eligible for Financial Aid to offset your costs. There are many different kinds of colleges, and the cost can vary greatly. If you have enrolled in a community college and plan to transfer to a university, you can often cut the cost of earning your Bachelor's degree by as much as 50%. Often if you qualify for Financial Aid, the greater your expenses, the more aid you'll receive. Never assume you can't afford to attend or transfer to a specific college. Always apply for Financial Aid, even if you think you are not eligible for assistance. Most students should plan on working part-time, and also asking their parents for financial support to cover their college expenses. Be prepared to take out student loans, as necessary, although don't take out loans just because it seems like easy money, as you'll have to pay back those loans with interest when you graduate or leave school! For ideas on how to earn money to cover your college expenses, see the list in Chapter 9, "Almost 100 Ways To Earn Money For College."

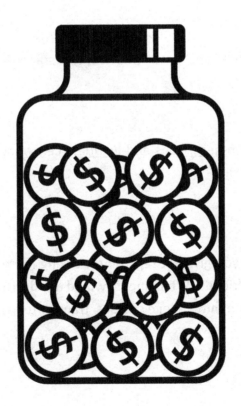

Money Management: Pat's Budget

Gas to & from school	$60 per month
Cell Phone	$50 per month
Textbooks	$450 per semester
Extra Large Café Mocha	$4.50 per day
Finishing your college degree-	PRICELESS!!!

Read the information about a community college student named Pat. Fill in the worksheet, and refer to it to answer the following questions:

Based on the information presented, what are Pat's total <u>expenses</u> this semester?

What is Pat's total <u>income</u> per semester?

Which of Pat's expenses are "fixed" (more or less stay the same each semester)?

Differentiate between <u>necessities</u> and <u>luxuries</u> (i.e., what Pat must buy versus what she could do without).

What advice would you give Pat regarding working more hours and moving into an apartment with her friends? What impact would this decision have on the time it takes Pat to finish her community college courses, transfer to a university, and complete her degree?

NOTE: FOR THIS ACTIVITY, A SEMESTER EQUALS 16 WEEKS (4 MONTHS)

- Pat pays an average of $450 each semester for textbooks.

- Community college tuition is $26 per unit of credit.
  Pat always enrolls in 15 units each semester.

- If Pat completes 2 classes each summer, she can meet her goal to transfer to a university within two years.

- Pat qualifies for a grant that covers her community college tuition each semester.

- Pat receives a scholarship for $250 each school year; it is renewable each year, but she must maintain a 2.5 GPA to keep it.

- Pat received a parking ticket twice this semester because she was running late from her job and she parked in a Faculty/Staff parking spot closer to her classroom (total fines = $50).

- Pat earns $230 per week at her job at a local restaurant; her take-home pay after taxes is $200.

- Pat's boss would like her to double her work hours from 15 to 30 per week; he'll pay her $8 per hour if she works more hours (Pat currently earn $7 per hour).

- Pat lives at home, so she doesn't have to pay any rent. However, her friends have been asking her to share an apartment with them (her share of the rent would be $300 per month).

- Pat spends about $60 per month on gas to get to and from school.

- Pat has been having trouble in her Chemistry class and is worried that if she does poorly in this class, her grade point average will drop below a 2.5.

- If Pat moves into an apartment with her friends, she can ride the bus to campus for a reduced student fee of $15 per month.

- Pat's significant other's birthday is coming up soon; she'd really like to buy him that $400 cell phone with all the neat options that he was admiring recently.

- Pat buys her lunch Monday - Friday at an average cost of $5 per day ($25 per week).

- Pat spends about $400 per semester on clothing.

- Pat plans to transfer to a university after two years, and she knows she will need to take out some loans to cover some of her expenses. She's trying to keep her total debt (student loans) under $15,000 for her Bachelor's Degree. So far, she hasn't had to take out any loans.

- Pat's car is pretty old, but she owns it; she could buy a new one for $300 per month.

- Pat likes to stop at The Coffee House Monday - Friday on her way to campus and buy the largest café mocha with an extra shot of espresso (cost = $4.50).

- Pat has been suffering from allergies; she thinks she should visit a doctor to get a prescription to get her through allergy season.

- Pat is still covered by her parents' health insurance, so doctor's visits are free; she must pay $10 for prescriptions.

- The college offers free tutoring Monday – Friday.

- Pat spends about $300 per month on her cell phone, auto insurance, personal necessities, and on entertainment (downloading music, going to the movies, and dining out with her friends).

- Pat would like to go on a nice vacation this summer.
  Estimated cost = $1000

- Pat could save $3 a day if she made her lunch instead of buying it.

- Pat's Academic Advisor has been encouraging her to cut back on her work hours so she can transfer to a university sooner.

- Pat has been promised a job as a Management Trainee at a starting salary of $30,000 per year- once she's finished her Bachelor's Degree.

- Pat spends $80 a month on getting her hair trimmed. She knows it's kind of expensive, but she really like the way her stylist cuts her hair.

- Pat's job has kept her from taking advantage of the college's free tutoring service, so she hired a private tutor to help her with Chemistry (cost = $20 per week).

PAT'S BUDGET

Worksheet

Income this semester:

Item	*Amount per semester*
Grants	_____
Scholarships	_____
Job	_____
Other	_____
TOTAL INCOME	_____

Expenditures this semester:

Item	*Amount per semester*	If this item is a NECESSITY check here	If this item is a LUXURY check here	If this item is a FIXED expense each semester check here
_____	_____	_____	_____	_____
_____	_____	_____	_____	_____
_____	_____	_____	_____	_____
_____	_____	_____	_____	_____
_____	_____	_____	_____	_____
_____	_____	_____	_____	_____
_____	_____	_____	_____	_____
_____	_____	_____	_____	_____
_____	_____	_____	_____	_____
_____	_____	_____	_____	_____
TOTAL EXPENDITURES	_____			

Answer the following questions:

Based on the information presented, what are Pat's total <u>expenses</u> this semester?

What is Pat's total <u>income</u> this semester?

Did Pat spend more money than she brought in from different sources this semester?

Which expenditures are "fixed" (more or less stay the same each semester)?

Which expenditures did you identify as LUXURIES? Which did you identify as NECESSITIES?

Where are some areas where Pat could cut back on spending each semester?

What are some expenses that Pat could eliminate in order to save money for a vacation this year?

How will Pat's budget be different if she moves into an apartment with her friends?

How much money does Pat potentially lose for each extra year it takes her to complete her Bachelor's Degree?

What advice would you give Pat regarding working more hours and moving into an apartment with her friends? What impact would this decision have on the time it takes Pat to finish her community college courses, transfer to a university, and complete her degree?

What are some strategies Pat could use to transfer to a university and complete her Bachelor's degree sooner?

YOUR OWN BUDGET

Outline **your** own budget for this semester. List all sources of income and all major expenditures.

<u>**Income this semester:**</u>

Item	*Amount <u>per semester</u>*
Grants	_____
Scholarships	_____
Job	_____
Other	_____
TOTAL INCOME	_____

<u>**Expenditures this semester:**</u>

Item Amount <u>per semester</u>		If this item is a NECESSITY check here	If this item is a LUXURY check here	If this item is a FIXED expense each semester check here
_____	_____	_____	_____	_____
_____	_____	_____	_____	_____
_____	_____	_____	_____	_____
_____	_____	_____	_____	_____
_____	_____	_____	_____	_____
_____	_____	_____	_____	_____
_____	_____	_____	_____	_____
_____	_____	_____	_____	_____

TOTAL EXPENDITURES   _____

Answer the following questions:

- What are your total <u>expenses</u> per semester?

- What is your total <u>income</u> per semester?

- Which expenses are "fixed"?

- Would eliminating any "luxury" items help your budget in any way?

- What did you learn from this exercise?

Case Study: The Laptop

Maria was excited about starting college. She had applied for financial aid and was informed she would receive enough money to cover her tuition and books. She also was eligible for a grant that would help her to pay for other expenses. She planned to save money by living at home and commuting to class, instead of living in the campus dorms. She knew if she also saved the money from her part-time job, she would be able to buy her own laptop computer. When school started Maria would go to the Computer Lab to use the computers. However, there was a two hour limit on the computers, and she sometimes had to wait almost an hour for a computer station to open up. She knew that if she bought her laptop she would no longer have to depend on the Computer Lab to write her papers and to do research on the Internet. She decided to move up the purchase date of her laptop; as soon as her next financial aid check arrived, she would go shopping for her own computer. She also planned on buying some new clothes so that she could "fit in" better at the college. Maria was concerned that her parents might try to dip into her financial aid funds, so she purposely tried to get to the mailbox before they did so they wouldn't know when her checks arrived or how much money she had in her account. One day Maria arrived home to see her mother sitting at the kitchen table paying the monthly bills. She could tell her mom was stressed out. On the table was an envelope from the Financial Aid Office- her check had arrived. She quickly scooped it up and tried to head down the hall to her room, when her mother stopped her. "Maria," she said, "We have to talk. They are going to shut off the electricity and I don't have enough money to pay the bill. I know they give you money for school and you have money from your job. I want you to give me some money to pay the electric bill." "But Mom," she protested, "I need that money to pay my school bills. I need to buy my own computer or I won't be able to keep up in my classes!" Her mother looked hurt and said "I don't think it's too much to ask you to help out with the bills. You live here yet you have never helped us out with any money." "Besides," she continued, "Your dad can pay you back when he gets his next check." Maria knew that

the chances of her dad paying her back were slim to none! He had never been very good at managing the family finances. Maria went to her room and shut the door. Maybe her mom was right- she should help out her family. Yet she had a sinking feeling that if she said yes this time, it would not be the last.

1)   Should Maria give her mother money to pay the electric bill?

2)   Is Maria's mother right to ask that she contribute to the family's finances?

3)   How can Maria help her family and still have enough money to buy her laptop?

4)   What will happen if Maria can't buy new clothes to fit in better at the college?

5)   If you were Maria, how would you handle this situation?

Problem Solving: John's Budget

At the end of his sophomore year, John, a student at State University decides to move out of the dorms and rent an apartment off campus with friends for his last two years of college. John has been paying $1300 per month for Room & Board (i.e., dorm fees and a cafeteria meal plan). He figures that moving off campus and cooking his own meals will cost less than living in the dorms and having to buy a cafeteria meal plan.

John and his two friends find an apartment that they can share for the next school year. The rent is $1200 per month. In addition to the rent, John and his roommates must pay a total of $90 per month for utilities, $90 per month tenant fees (which includes access to the swimming pool in the apartment complex) and $150 per month to have their apartment cleaned. John is a good cook, and has offered to prepare dinner every night if each of his roommates will each pay 40% of the total food bill, which is $1000 per month for all three; his housemates like this option.

John knows he could save money if he were to prepare his own sack lunches and take them to campus every day (it would cost him $3 per day to make his own lunch). However, John doesn't really like to prepare his lunch in advance- he prefers cooking dinner for everyone. John decides he will buy lunch on campus 7 days per week, which will run approximately $8 per day ($6 for a sandwich or entrée, and $2 per day for a drink). Every afternoon John also stops by the Campus Café to buy a cup of coffee and a snack. He figures the cost for this is about $5 per day. If he were to take his own snacks to school, he would save about $3 per day.

Use the following to calculate John's monthly expenses:

Current Scenario: *Living on Campus*

Item	Cost
Room & board	$1300/m
TOTAL	$1300/mo

Scenario 2:   *Living in an Apartment & cooking for housemates*

Item	Cost
Rent	_____
Utilities	_____
Tenant Fees	_____
House Cleaning	_____
Food – groceries	_____
Lunches	_____
Snacks	_____
TOTAL	_____

Scenario 3:   *Living in an Apartment & cooking for housemates & preparing own lunch and snacks to take to school*

Item	Cost
Rent	_____
Utilities	_____
Tenant Fees	_____
House Cleaning	_____
Food – groceries	_____
Lunches	_____
Snacks	_____
TOTAL	_____

Answer the following questions:

1) How much will John spend on food each month, given the cooking arrangements he has worked out with his roommates (including the amount of money he spends buying his lunches and purchasing snacks each day)?

2) How much money could John save each month by packing his own lunch and taking snacks from home?

3) If John earns $8 per hour (after taxes and deductions) at his part-time job, how many extra hours must he work per month to pay for the additional expenses he has due to buying his lunch and afternoon snacks on campus?

4) If John's housemates decide that they don't want John to cook for them, what will John's share of the monthly food bill be?

5) Does John save money by moving out of the dorm and into an apartment with his friends? If so, how much per month?

6) What are some other ways John and his housemates can save money each month?

Self-Assessment

Rate yourself on the behaviors of successful students on a scale of 1 – 5. How well prepared are you in the following areas?

    1 = I need lots of help with this

    2 = I could do better in this area

    3 = I'm OK in this area

    4 = I do a good job in this area

    5 = I'm very good at this

MONEY MANAGEMENT

____   I have a budget that I refer to each school year to help me manage my money

____   I know how to apply for Financial Aid, as well as the deadlines to apply each year

____   I apply for scholarships for which I am eligible

____   I consciously try to avoid accumulating student debt (i.e., I avoid taking out student loans unless absolutely necessary)

____   I understand the terms of repayment for any student loans I take out, including the amount I am borrowing, the interest rate, when I have to start making payments, how much my monthly payments will be, how many years I will have to pay back the loan, and the total amount I will end up paying back with interest

____   I work at an outside job during school breaks to earn money to pay school expenses

____   I know how to keep my transportation costs to a minimum

____   I plan my driving trips in advance so that I run multiple errands at one time (and cut down on the amount of gas I have to purchase)

____   Before I make a purchase or attend a social event, I make sure I have enough money in my budget to pay for it

___ I know the difference between purchases that are necessities versus luxuries

___ I don't get hit with unexpected expenses (such as paying the tab for others when I go out or paying for parking tickets)

___ I save money by planning my meals, preparing my own lunch, and shopping accordingly

___ I am familiar with ways to cut down on my book expenses (e.g. buying used textbooks, renting textbooks, selling textbooks that I no longer need)

___ I have money in a savings account that I can tap when unexpected expenses come up

___ I have a low-cost copy card that I use to minimize the cost of photocopying materials

___ I take advantage of free campus services such as tutoring and counseling

___ I know how to go online to research the cost of my books for each semester, and to compare costs by purchasing them through different sources

Place a checkmark next to any items that you rated a 1 (I need lots of help with this) or a 2 (I could do better in this area). Identify where you could go on campus in order to solicit help and learn more about these areas.

The following ideas can help you to manage your money in college.

- Keep a regular budget and note even small purchases in an electronic file or small notebook.

- Meet with Financial Aid representatives before taking on any student loan debt to ensure that you are aware of how much money you will have to pay back and when your payments will begin.

- Consider walking, biking, taking public transit or carpooling with others to keep your transportation costs down.

- Check your college's website to answer questions you have about Financial Aid including application deadlines and available scholarships.

- If you live off campus, consider preparing your own meals and packing a sack lunch so that you aren't tempted to eat out every day. Shop around to see which local stores offer the best prices on the items you consistently buy.

- Talk to other students to learn about ways to save money on textbook purchases. Consider purchasing used textbooks or online versions of textbooks to save money.

- Know the difference between a necessity (something you must have) and a luxury (something you don't have to have, but would like to have). Make sure you have enough money in your budget to cover all major expenses each school year, and know how much money you can spend each week or month on non-necessities.

- Avoid paying for services that you can get for free on campus.

- Take advantage of on-campus jobs and summer employment opportunities to build up your savings

Chapter Notes:

Things to think about...

Things to remember...

Things to do....

Chapter 7

Strategies For Winning
The College Game

*"Alone we can do so little,
together we can do so much."*

Helen Keller

Your Learning Style- Make It Work For You!

Have you ever thought about how you prefer to learn new material? Some students enjoy listening to lectures in large classes with hundreds of other students. Others prefer a more active learning environment such as a laboratory where they can "roll up their sleeves and get their hands dirty" doing experiments or testing different hypotheses. Some students prefer to absorb new material through reading and highlighting their textbooks, or developing research or term papers. Many students prefer a combination of approaches to learning.

Each of us has a preferred style of learning, or preferred styles, and no one style is better than the others. You may already clearly know your preferred learning style, or this may be the first time you have actively thought about your learning preferences. What's important to understand is: A) your own learning preference, B) the way you prefer to learn does not always match your college professors' style of teaching, and C) techniques you can use to help the learning process when your learning style is different than the way your professors teach. Knowing your learning style can help you to understand why you prefer certain types of classes and professors over others, as well as why you may tend to do better in certain types of classes. This information can also help you to learn to build on your strengths, and figure out techniques to address your weaknesses. It is also helpful to know the learning styles of your classmates when you are working together in a study group. This way, if you do not share the same dominant learning style, you can figure out ways to present the material to others using a different learning style.

According to "Learning Styles Explained" (LDPride.net), the three main types of learning styles are Visual, Auditory, and Kinesthetic or Tactile.

People who are **Visual** learners learn best by seeing (e.g., the teacher's facial expressions and body language). They prefer classes where visual aids are used, such as pictures, charts, and maps. They are good at taking notes, and prefer written assignments over verbal presentations.

People who are **Auditory** learners learn best by listening. They prefer classes where they listen to lectures and music, or participate in group discussions. They can benefit from recording lectures and reading material aloud. They prefer verbal presentations over written reports or presentations.

People who are **Kinesthetic** learners learn best through movement and touching materials. They prefer classes that are hands-on, such as labs where they conduct experiments.

Knowing your preferred learning style can help you to succeed in college. If you know you are more of a Kinesthetic or hands-on learner, you may opt for a college or university, or choose a major that emphasizes "learn by doing." You would also be wise to try to avoid courses where you must sit through hours of your professors lecturing while you only take notes. If you acquire information best by listening, or you are an Auditory learner, you won't be deterred from taking lecture classes, and may really enjoy classes where you engage in discussions with your classmates, or where you listen to music or poetry readings. (Note: Most college professors seem to prefer lecturing as the primary way to teach their students, which is good news if you are an Auditory learner). If you learn best visually, or you are a Visual learner, you may find yourself drawn to art classes or classes in drama, TV or video production. Visual learners learn best through visual displays, such as PowerPoint outlines, video clips, charts and graphs.

To help identify your preferred learning style, complete the following section.

Place a checkmark next to each statement that applies to you:

Section A

____ I prefer classes where I can work with manipulatives or build models.

____ I find that pacing or moving around when I am studying helps me to retain information.

____ I would rather go on a nature hike than read a book about nature.

____ I love classes that incorporate structured learning experiences such as case studies or simulations.

____ I find myself daydreaming when I have to sit in class for a long time.

____ I am good at working with my hands and building models.

____ I enjoy classes that have a physical element to them such as exercise or movement.

____ I'd rather have a job where I go out in the field to work, than to sit and work in an office.

____ I prefer a college with the motto "Learn by doing" versus one that emphasizes theoretical learning.

____ I like to flip through my textbooks to get a feel for them before I start reading them.

TOTAL number of checkmarks for Section A = ___

Section B

____ I enjoy classes where students participate in smaller discussion groups to review the material.

____ I prefer classes where the primary mode of relaying information is lecture.

____ I recite information aloud when I am studying to help me remember it.

____ I believe it is important to pay attention to an instructor's voice to understand what they are really saying.

___ I have been known to record class sessions so I can refer back to the material at a later time.

___ I enjoy listening to audio versions of books or listening to lectures I have downloaded.

___ I would rather tell a friend about my summer vacation than show them pictures of my trip.

___ In order to find a building on campus, I would rather someone tell me where it is than show me a campus map.

___ I would rather listen to music than watch a movie.

___ I'd rather attend a class lecture than a class laboratory.

TOTAL number of checkmarks for Section B = ___

Section C

___ I like to use flash cards to memorize material such as new vocabulary words.

___ I learn best by taking lots of notes in class or while reading my textbooks.

___ I love to highlight my textbooks to help me learn new material.

___ I like to sit near the front of the class so I can see the teacher's face.

___ I find it helps me to learn if my instructor uses a PowerPoint presentation, or some other kind of visual display.

___ I like discussion groups where someone records the information on a flipchart or on a white board.

___ In order to help me remember something, I try to see a picture of it in my mind.

___ I like classes where the instructor shows video clips or movies.

___ I post notes to myself on my wall or mirror to help me remember things I need to do.

___ I always include pictures or diagrams about my subject whenever I have to give a class presentation.

TOTAL number of checkmarks for Section C = ___

Determine which style you rely on the most when learning by adding up the number of items you checked in each category. If you had more checkmarks in Section A, you are likely a **KINESTHETIC LEARNER**. If you had more checkmarks in Section B, you are likely a **VISUAL LEARNER**. If you had more checkmarks in Section C, you are likely an **AUDITORY LEARNER**. Remember, you can have more than one learning style or preference.

Some students think that they should avoid certain majors or classes where the primary method of relaying information is different than their preferred learning style. Perhaps you are interested in literature classes, yet know that reading for hours on end is not your favorite way to learn. Does this mean you should never sign up for a literature class? Not necessarily. If you can find a way to build on your learning strengths, such as listening to recorded versions of books, or attending dramatic performances based on the books you are studying, you may find yourself enjoying literature courses that you might have initially avoided. A novice student might give up easily and decide never to take a literature class. A more seasoned problem solver would investigate ways to accomplish his or her goals, despite initial feelings that the goal is unattainable.

Once you identify your learning style, you can figure out which tools to use to help your own studying. For example, if you are a visual learner, you might want to convert your notes from a lecture class (auditory format) to index cards to review, or to posters of diagrams and drawings you can tape to your wall and review daily. Sometimes you can't avoid taking courses taught by professors whose teaching style does not match your learning style, so you must then figure out how to make the learning environment work for you. See the tips on the following pages for ideas for how to convert material into a format that works best for you.

Answer the following questions:

I am primarily a _____ learner.

I know this because I:

I prefer the following learning strategies:

TIPS FOR VISUAL LEARNERS

Sit close to the instructor or the white board so you can see everything clearly

Use plenty of visual aids

Group items by color (color coding)

Use highlighters to mark up your textbooks and notes

Summarize your notes (answer the question "In other words" or, "In a nutshell" or "What the author really means is...")

Create study flashcards to learn new vocabulary words or a foreign language (however, don't put too much on each card – it clutters the mental picture you will have)

Write explanations next to diagrams

Write out the steps to completing a math problem

Use your laptop/tablet! Type your notes and printout study sheets to review later

Use post-it notes

Check out videos, maps and charts from the library

Redraw the diagrams in your textbooks

Keep your study area quiet

Use symbols & pictures to help you remember important information

Make charts to organize information

Keep a supply of graph paper for charts and diagrams

Reorganize your notes using your PC – e.g., create spreadsheets or tables

TIPS FOR KINESTHETIC LEARNERS

Learn by doing

Study with music playing in the background

Set up a comfortable study area

Take lots of study breaks

Get involved in hands-on activities (e.g., labs, building competitions, dramatic performances)

Use physical activity to reinforce learning (e.g., walk while you memorize vocabulary)

Choose a seat near the front of the lecture hall so you aren't distracted by others

Sign up for classes where you learn through using case studies or role playing

Participate in field trips

Rewrite or type your notes and refer back to them when studying

Use flash cards

Talk with your hands (move your hands as you speak)

Build a model illustrating a key concept

Use post-it notes; arrange them in sequence

Use a whiteboard or flipcharts to post notes

Use your laptop (typing is tactile)

Listen to your recorded notes while you exercise

Build on your ability to work well with tools and to play musical instruments

TIPS FOR AUDITORY LEARNERS

Set up your learning environment so you can clearly hear the lecture or speaker

Take in information through the radio or TV

Read instructions or textbook materials aloud

Participate in group discussions

Listen to CD's, or download books or recorded lectures

Imagine hearing the instructor explain the material

Sign up for classes where you can talk in class and interact with others

Quiz others verbally

Speak out loud while you study, especially when memorizing information

Use music, singing and rhymes to help you retain information

Record lectures (only listen to the parts of the lecture that were confusing to keep this from being overly time-consuming)

Rephrase the problem using your own words

Take advantage of opportunities to be graded based on oral presentations or oral exams

Build on your ability to learn other languages quickly

Join a study group where the course material will be discussed

List a subject that you are currently studying or plan to study soon:

What are the typical tools or strategies you would use to try to learn the material (e.g., read the textbook, highlight key phrases, create study cards)?

What are some other tools or strategies you could use to learn this subject, especially if the instructor tends to teach in a style that is different than your dominant learning style?

How To Avoid Academic Probation

There are some things you will want to avoid in college, such as overloading your schedule, running out of money, and being placed on Academic Probation. At some colleges even students who have a high GPA can end up on Academic Probation due to dropping too many classes or not completing enough units each quarter or semester. Check your college catalog for general information on what is required to stay in good academic standing so that you don't receive a surprise letter at some point in your academic career informing you that you are on Academic Probation and that corrective action is necessary.

If your GPA drops below a 2.0 (C average) in college, or you frequently enroll in classes and then drop them, you may find yourself on Academic Probation. The following information may help you avoid being placed on Academic Probation, or may be of assistance should you find yourself on Academic Probation. Unfortunately, many students find themselves on Academic Probation each semester. The reasons for this vary, but often include:

* Enrolling in too many units in a given semester or quarter

* Working too many hours at a job while attending school

* Being embarrassed to ask for tutorial assistance when encountering academic difficulty

* Enrolling in a course without having completed required prerequisite courses

* Dropping one or more courses after the drop deadline for the semester or quarter

There may be two or more types of Academic Probation at your college or university, such as:

General Academic Probation: Typically, students whose GPA falls below a 2.0 are placed on Academic Probation. Being placed on Probation more than a certain number of semesters, may result in the student being dismissed from the college.

Progress Probation: Students who frequently sign up for classes and do not complete them (i.e., they drop them or earn Incomplete or No Credit grades) may end up on Progress Probation.

If you do end up being placed on Academic Probation, the following strategies may help you to get back in good standing with your college or university:

- Consider repeating courses you have previously taken in order to improve your GPA. Consult with an Academic Advisor for questions related to repeating courses (some colleges and universities place limits on the number of times a course can be repeated).

- If you repeat courses, check with the Registrar's Office to see if you must file Repeat Cards so that your GPA is adjusted on your transcripts.

- Check to see if your campus has an Academic Renewal policy which will enable you to have poor grades deleted from your GPA if you meet certain conditions.

- Avail yourself of free tutoring services provided by your college. Don't wait until you experience academic difficulty in a course to seek help.

- Consider cutting back on either the number of units you take each semester, the number of hours you work, or extracurricular activities. Generally, full-time students (i.e., taking 12 or more units) are encouraged to work no more than 15 - 20 hours per week. Students who work full-time (40 hours per week) are encouraged to enroll in college on a part-time basis (no more than 3-6 units per semester). You should plan on at least 2 hours of homework and study time for each hour you are in class. Thus, a student taking 15 units would need approximately 30 hours per week to study in order to remain in good standing with the college, i.e., avoid being placed on Academic Probation.

- Schedule an appointment to meet with an Academic Advisor to review your progress to date and to develop a realistic Educational Plan. Advisors can help you to identify problem areas, and brainstorm solutions to overcome academic difficulties.

KEY CONCEPT: Smart students know when to ask for help.

Effective Note-taking

Wouldn't it be great if you could just go to your college classes, sit back comfortably and listen to your instructor lecture, and somehow magically retain all that information- *and* be able to recall it when it comes time for final exams? Unfortunately, most of us don't have a photographic memory and we have to find some other way to capture information during class. Taking notes during lectures or class sessions is the first step in committing the content of your courses to memory. There's something about physically writing your notes or typing them on your laptop computer or notepad (both kinesthetic acts), seeing the writing on the paper (a visual act), and then rereading them aloud (an auditory act) that helps you to recall the information later when you need it.

There are different styles or methods of note-taking. The most common methods are the <u>Outline Method</u>, the <u>Cornell Method</u>, and the <u>Mind Map Method</u>. Check online or with the staff at your college or university's Library, Tutoring, or Study Skills Center for more information about these methods and other ways to take effective notes. Only you can decide which method works best for you. Some students hurriedly try to write down *every word* the professor says, and end up not really hearing or understanding what is being said (they're too busy taking notes). Others take notes, but don't know what to do with them after the class session ends. Some students take notes, but then can't decipher what they wrote, because their handwriting is too hard to read.

Today's college students have access to many tools to help them organize their notes and turn them into useful study aids. Some students take advantage of formal note-taking services, i.e., they subscribe to a service where students who have successfully completed a course sit in on the classes and take notes, and then share them electronically with other students for a fee.

Tips To Help You Get The Most Out Of Your Notes

- Make sure you have the proper supplies: A clean notebook, pens or pencils in different colors, a good writing surface, a highlighter, or a laptop or tablet that's charged up and ready to go. Use a separate notebook or binder for each course you are taking.

- Spend some time reading the chapters in your textbook that will be covered in upcoming lectures. Think about the material and note things that catch your attention, or questions you have about the material. During class, listen for the answers to your questions.

- If something is not clear, ask your classmates to see if they will share their understanding of the material with you, or visit your professor during his/her office hours to ask for clarification.

- Eliminate distractions. Turn off your cell phone and put it away in your backpack. Make it a point to sit where you will have a good view of the instructor. Avoid sitting with friends if they tend to chat during class and distract you from the lecture.

- Type up your notes, or reformat them and brainstorm questions that you think might be on an upcoming test. Print out small study cards with a question at the top, and a short answer below or on the reverse side. If you need to memorize lots of terms or pictures, print these out on study cards and carry them with you so you can review them while eating lunch, waiting for the bus, or other times when you have a few free minutes. All those little study times will add up, making your preparation for final exams easier.

- Try to focus on how the material from this class will set the stage for learning in other classes. If this is the only class of its type you will take, and you think the material is boring, challenge yourself to make the learning more interesting by connecting the information to something that is relevant to you (e.g., a problem you have faced, something related to your future career).

- Make up your own shorthand to speed up note-taking. Leave out vowels, use pictures or symbols, or write abbreviations of words. If you're making up unusual abbreviations or symbols for certain things, write a key at the top of the page noting what each symbol means to avoid any confusion later.

- Size up your instructors early in the semester to gain an understanding of how they lecture. Do they talk nonstop throughout the class? You might want to record the lectures for later referral, if necessary. Do they encourage the students to engage in discussion? If so, you might want to take notes on your fellow classmates' responses. Do they show video clips? Make a note of the title or the web address so you can review it later on your own.

- At the end of each lecture, write down 5 "learnings" or key points you want to remember.

- If your professor uses big words or lots of technical terms that can be confusing, take some time after class to rewrite your notes in laymen's terms (i.e., pretend you are explaining the material to a friend, but use words you would normally use in your daily conversations). Tell yourself, "What she really meant was…" or "What he's really trying to say is…"

- Write a note on the cover of each of your notebooks- "REWARD – If lost please return to …" and include your name, phone number and email address. If you accidentally leave a notebook in a big lecture hall or the library towards the end of the semester, giving someone a gift card for coffee is a small price to pay for having all your valuable notes returned to you.

*I once worked with a student who confided that he would start thinking about a particular point in a lecture, and get so absorbed in trying to figure out that one thing that he would miss the rest of the lecture. I suggested that as he was taking notes, he should list questions he had in the margins so that he could go back to them after the class session to follow-up. If this happens to you during a lecture, something as quick as drawing a big question mark next to portions of your notes can signal that you weren't clear on what the professor was saying and need to go back later to clarify this.

Think about how you have taken notes in the past (in high school or previous college courses).

Describe how you normally take notes:

Are they legible and organized?

Do you take lots of notes, or write down only key points?

How effective have your notes been in the past when it comes time to recall the information or prepare for exams?

How soon do you review your notes after you have taken them?

Is there anything you would like to change about the way you take notes to make the process more effective?

Preparing For Tests

Like them or not, tests are an ongoing part of college life. If you're well-prepared and acing all your classes, taking tests is probably no big deal. But if you're like many college students, taking tests is probably one of your least favorite aspects of college life. Tests can be cumulative in nature (you're tested on everything you learned at the end of the semester or quarter), or can be offered throughout the

semester in the form of quizzes, midterm exams and final exams. Some exams are "take-home," and some are even open book (you get to refer to your textbook or notes during the test). Others may be taken online in a timed setting. Some classes may require a long research paper as the final exam, or even a series of essays. As with other aspects of college life, you can go into testing situations not knowing what to expect and feeling panicked, or you can take some time to prepare for upcoming exams and walk in with more confidence.

Think back to some tests you had to take in the past. Do you conjure up images of shaking your head in fear, or do you have memories of having done well on exams? The fact that you are in college means you are probably very experienced at taking tests. Think of test-taking as a skill that you can improve. If you know a certain professor gives a cumulative final to determine students' grades, yet you prefer to be graded on a group of projects or assignments, you would be wise to steer clear of courses taught by this professor. To find out how different professors grade and test their students, ask other students who have taken their classes before. If you love writing and the idea of crafting a 20 page research paper sounds appealing, then you may want to take a class from professors who grade based on this option. If test-taking is a skill, then becoming aware of how different professors test their students is a strategy you can use when selecting your classes. As with other skills, the more you practice, the better you (usually) become at it. So your freshman year of college may be a bit nerve-wrecking as you find out what to expect for exams. However, by your senior year of college, test-taking will probably be easier for you, or at least not as scary as when you started college.

It's important that you see tests for what they are – a measure of how you did on an exam at a specific point in time. Doing well on tests does not mean you are better than someone who does not do well on tests- it may just mean you're a better test-taker, or you spent more time preparing for the test. To put tests in perspective, ask yourself, "What is the worst thing that could happen if I don't do well on this exam?" As my favorite teacher used to say, "Ask yourself, 'Am I still alive? Does my mother still love me? Will the sun come up tomorrow?'" and if the answer to these questions is "yes," then you can move on if you don't do well on an exam. Luckily, many colleges allow students to retake classes if they don't do well the first time around. While you don't want to make a habit of repeating classes (and there may be limits on the number of times you can repeat a class), knowing your options can help to keep you calm and focused during testing situations.

Here are some tips for preparing for exams:

- Start preparing for exams the first week of classes. Review your notes weekly, and make study cards that you flip through during breaks between classes or when you have a few minutes of free time. Trying to memorize huge quantities of information may be overwhelming, but breaking your studying into smaller bits makes it more manageable.

- Don't wait until you're doing poorly in a class to ask for help. At the first sign of academic difficulty, find out if tutoring is available on campus in that subject. Many colleges offer free tutoring services to enrolled students.

- Keep up with the required reading. If you have 24 chapters to read in a 12 week quarter, you'll probably have to read at least 2 chapters per week to stay caught up.

- Don't pull "all-nighters." Make sure you get enough sleep the night before an exam. Do this by studying throughout the semester. Cramming for exams at the last minute may enable you to slide by, but it puts too much pressure on you and doesn't help you to retain the information on a long-term basis.

- If you feel anxious during tests, make an appointment with a Counselor or Psychologist at the campus Health Center or Counseling & Psychological Services Center to discuss strategies for dealing with and preventing this.

- Sometimes old tests are available for students to review. Make sure that doing so is OK with your instructor so as not to violate any academic integrity policies (i.e., be guilty of cheating). Sometimes just knowing the format of the tests a particular instructor gives can save you time during the test. This is also very helpful when taking big standardized tests that are required for admission to college or graduate school.

- Spend a few minutes sizing up each test before you start. Look at the number of problems or questions you must answer and consider the amount of time you have to complete to pace yourself during the exam.

- If you suspect that you may have a Learning Disability that is affecting your performance on exams, or you are so paralyzed by fear during exams that you can't complete them, schedule an appointment with a Counselor or staff member at your college's Disabled Student Services Department. A skilled professional can help you to determine if you do have a disability and assist you in getting the proper accommodations (such as increased time for taking tests).

- Have faith that you have all the resources to accomplish whatever it is that you are supposed to do in life (and therefore cheating to get a good grade on a test is not necessary). Be flexible in adjusting your life and career goals, and even your major, if necessary. If you want to be a surgeon, but faint whenever you have to get a shot, or get queasy dissecting specimens during your Biology or Anatomy labs, you should probably rethink your career goals.

- Focus on using test preparation strategies that are consistent with your learning preferences. If you are a Visual Learner, use lots of pictures, graphs and images to prepare for tests. If you are more of an Auditory Learner, recite your notes aloud when preparing for tests. If you are a Kinesthetic Learner, try to build models or use physical movement (such as pacing when studying) to help you remember material.

**KEY CONCEPT: In college you learn how to learn
(which prepares you for a lifetime of learning).**

Think about how you have prepared for quizzes, tests, or exams in the past, and answer the following questions:

What worked?

What didn't work?

Make a commitment to increasing the behaviors that helped you to do well and avoid those things that did not help.

How many exams will you have to take this semester or quarter? Build extra study time in your schedule the week or two before each exam. Set study goals and develop a schedule to review material. Pencil the dates of upcoming quizzes and exams below, then plug this information into your daily planner or electronic calendar, and send reminders to yourself about upcoming tests.

Course Title	Quizzes	Midterm Exam	Final Exam
Psych 1	10/1, 12/1	11/1	12/15

Take The Initiative To Learn More

Successful students aren't afraid to ask for help. If you need assistance in any of the following areas, check your college website or campus kiosks or bulletin boards, or ask your academic advisor if s/he knows where you can attend free campus workshops on these topics:

Memorization Techniques

How do you approach the task of memorizing material? Do you have specific strategies? Do you have trouble recalling important information at exam time? Attend a campus workshop or do an Internet search to learn more about how to improve your memory.

Dealing With Test Anxiety

Do you walk into your exam session feeling well-prepared, but then you go blank when it's time to start the test? You may be dealing with Test Anxiety. See if your campus Counseling Center offers any workshops on how to ease those test jitters so you can perform better on exams.

How To Study For Tests

Could you benefit from learning more tools to study effectively? Learn how to create study cards from your textbook material, review material in manageable chunks, and plan ahead for tests by attending a workshop on this topic.

Accessing Library Resources

The library is a great place to study and to get help with research papers. Learn how to work with reference materials and online resources, and how to avoid plagiarism by checking out one of the many workshops your college Library is sure to offer.

Career Center Resources

Stop by your campus Career Center if you need assistance with developing your resume, learning how to interview for jobs effectively, obtaining job internships, or looking for summer employment.

Chapter Notes:

Things to think about...

Things to remember...

Things to do....

Chapter 8

Play Fair, Play Well

"College should shake you up a little, get you breathing, quicken your senses and animate a conscious examination of life's enduring questions."

William J. Bennett

Academic Integrity

Myth #9 - It doesn't matter if you cheat in college.

With the stakes being so high (a college degree, high paying jobs after graduation) it can be very tempting to cheat in college. Why do students cheat? You might see other students doing it, and think, "Well, they're cheating, so I might as well so the same." It's important to know that colleges take cheating very seriously. Your college Catalog most likely has information on what is considered cheating (plagiarism, copying research papers off of the Internet, not giving credit to proper sources when repeating ideas or information, copying during tests, etc.).

You can be dropped from a class for cheating and have to repeat it, or you can even get kicked out of college. If you're kicked out of college, this will most likely be noted on your transcripts, and that information will follow you to the next school you attend or apply to, and could follow you later to the job market where employers might ask to see copies of your transcripts.

While some students may be able to cheat their way through school, sooner or later this will catch up with them. What you actually learn in college (the content or skills) is what is really important. If you cheat in your classes, you may later find yourself in a job or a situation where you can't fake your way through it. Sometimes students cheat because they feel like that's the only way they can pass a class. If you are having trouble in a class, seek out tutorial assistance, form a study group with other students in your class, or visit your professor during his/her office hours to ask questions about the material. If you get the help you need throughout the semester, you are less likely to be tempted to cheat. By keeping up with your studies or starting to write research papers well before they are due (i.e., don't procrastinate until the last minute) you will more likely be prepared for exams and have sufficient time to write essays and research papers.

Plagiarism Scenarios

The* UCLA website lists the following examples of academic dishonesty:

1)   **Cheating**

2)   **Plagiarizing:** claiming someone's words or ideas as your own

3)   **Multiple Submissions:** submitting the same work for more than one class without permission

4)   **Fabricating:** making up or altering information/data

5)   **Facilitating:** helping someone engage in academic dishonesty

Using this list, decide which offense(s), if any, the students in the following scenarios committed.

—	John	*buying a research paper*
—	Jane	*copying someone else's exam*
—	Susie	*allowing someone else to copy her work*
—	Joe's classmates	*completing the homework together*
—	Alice	*incomplete footnotes & bibliography*
—	Betty	*making up sociology survey*
—	Bob	*resubmitting an old assignment as new*

*http://www/library.ucla.edu/bruinsuccess

Scenario #1

John has a research paper due next week. He hasn't started to write it yet because he has been working extra hours to pay for his college expenses. If he doesn't earn enough money, he won't be able to pay for college. If he keeps working overtime, he won't be able to write his paper. John has heard that there are some places he can look on the Internet where he can "buy" a paper on just about any topic. He is tempted to do this because he doesn't think he can pull this assignment off without some kind of help. He's sure that he would only so this one time- he doesn't plan to make it a habit.

What should John do?

How could John have avoided being in this situation?

Is it OK for John to cheat if it's only one time?

Scenario #2

Jane has been struggling in her History class. Jane's best friend, Susie, is doing really well in History. They both are in the same class. The professor likes to give multiple choice exams. Susie feels sorry for Jane and has offered to sit next to her during the upcoming exam so Jane can copy Susie's answers. If Jane can pass this class, she and Susie can transfer to the local university next semester together.

What should Jane do?

What should Susie do?

Is it worth cheating on the exam so the two friends can transfer to a university at the same time?

Is Susie really helping Jane by allowing her to copy from her exam? If yes, how so? If no, why not?

Scenario #3

Joe is taking a chemistry class. The professor grades on a curve and does not allow students to confer with each other when completing homework. Joe found out a group of three students regularly meet and do the homework together.

What should Joe do?

-    Ignore the students who are violating the class policy on homework assignments.

-    Report the three students to the professor.

-    Ask the group of students if he can join in with them when they meet so he can complete his homework with them.

-    Send an anonymous complaint to the Vice President of Student Services about the cheating that is taking place on campus.

-    Confront the three classmates and tell them if they don't stop conferring on the homework he will report them to the professor.

What are the advantages and/or disadvantages of each of the proposed responses?

Scenario #4

Alice is writing a paper and has had to spend a great amount of time citing the sources she reviewed in order to complete the assignment. Alice hates all of the work involved in listing footnotes and developing her Bibliography. She is thinking about only listing half of the footnotes and sources this time. She figures her professor won't notice because there are over 100 students in this class.

What should Alice do?

What are the chances the professor will find out that she did not cite her sources completely?

If she knew for sure that the professor wouldn't find out that she omitted required information, is it worth it to go ahead and submit her paper without giving credit to her sources?

Is it really plagiarism if Alice doesn't list all of her resources (as long as she gives credit for direct quotes that she includes)?

Scenario #5

Betty loves attending community college. She is involved in Student Government and in sports. She takes 18 units each semester so she can transfer to a university as soon as possible. She also works 30 hours per week on campus in the Financial Aid Office. Betty is supposed to interview 30 students as part of a Sociology assignment. She is so swamped with everything she's doing that she decides to interview only 10 students, and pretend to do the rest of the interviews. She knows so many students that she figures she can piece together the remaining 20 interviews based on other students she knows through school, work, and extracurricular activities.

Is it OK for Betty to make-up information as part of her assignment?

If yes, how so? If no, why not?

What advice would you give to Betty to help her avoid the temptation to cheat in her classes?

Scenario #6

Bob is a very bright student. He learns new material easily, and he is earning all A's in his college classes. Bob wishes his instructors would pick up the pace a little. Sometimes he feels bored because the classes don't move fast enough for him. One of Bob's Political Science professors just gave an assignment that is very similar to one he did last year in another Poli Sci class. Bob is thinking of cutting and pasting from the old assignment and turning it in as a new assignment. He figures he already understands the material, so why start from scratch on this assignment? He doesn't think he has anything to gain by doing the assignment all over again.

What should Bob do?

– Tell his instructor that the class is not challenging enough.

– Do a really good job of copying off of the old assignment so no one can tell he didn't complete the new assignment from scratch.

– Do the assignment anyway because he can probably still learn something.

Is Bob cheating if he copies material from one assignment to use for another assignment, if the first assignment was his own original work?

Mid-Semester Questionnaire

It would be ideal to complete the following activity during your first semester or year in college. However, even if you have been enrolled at your college or university for a while, you can still benefit from taking some time to think about your overall experience, which services you would like to investigate further, the behaviors that are supporting your academic success, and how you can make the most of your college years.

This questionnaire is designed to help you assess how you are doing at the mid-point of your first semester or first year in college. It will provide you the opportunity to reflect on your overall experience thus far. Answer the following questions:

1)　Is this your first semester in college?

　　If not, how many semesters have you attended college?

2)　At this point in time, what is your long-term goal (career or academic)?

3)　Have you decided on a major? If yes, what have you selected?

4)　On a scale of 1 - 10 (1 = terrible and 10 = outstanding), how would you rate your overall college experience so far?

5)　What do you like most about your college/university?

6)   If there was anything you could change about your college or university, what would it be?

7)   Complete the sentence: College is different than high school in the following way...

8)   Where is the best place on campus to study?

9)   Which campus service would you like to know more about?

10)   Have you met with an academic advisor yet?

11)   How long do you think it will take you to complete your academic degree or meet your goal (e.g., vocational training, university transfer, or degree)?

12)   Is there anything that is getting in the way of you meeting your academic or career goal in a timely manner?

13)   How have your classes been overall in terms of difficulty- too easy, too hard, or just right?

14)   Do you feel you are adequately prepared to do well in your college courses? If yes, what has helped you to be prepared? If no, what would help you to successfully complete your classes this semester and be better prepared for future courses you will take?

15)   Have you been actively participating in your classes (e.g., group discussions, asking questions, visiting your professors during office hours)? If yes, give an example. If no, what would make it easier for you to actively participate in class sessions?

16)   Are there any courses where you feel you could use tutoring support? If yes, have you visited any campus tutorial labs on campus to request assistance? If no, do you know what type of tutoring services are available at your campus?

17)   Have you met and interacted with students who come from different backgrounds than yourself (ethnic, socioeconomic, religious, political, etc.)?

If yes, what was that like?

If no, what could help you to meet and interact with students who are different from you?

18) Are you participating in any study groups?

If yes, who organized the group?

Has the study group been beneficial?

What is working well in the study group?

What should change, if anything, to make the study group better?

If no, do you think participating in a study group could be helpful to you?

Would you be willing to talk to your classmates to start a study group?

19) How much time have you spent this semester in the campus Library?

If more than 10 hours, how do you spend your time there?

If less than 10 hours, what would encourage you to spend more time there?

20)   Have you participated in any extracurricular activities on campus (e.g., clubs, sports, student government, theatre or musical events)?

If yes, what did you attend? Did you enjoy the event/activity?

If no, what would make it easier for you to get involved in campus activities?

21)   Do you see yourself taking on a leadership role on campus someday (e.g., participating in student government, organizing a club, getting involved in campus events)?

22)   What are 5 things you want to do before you graduate from college?

Making the Most of General Education

At some point in your college career you will most likely have to complete some "General Education" or "Breadth" courses. These can be courses in a variety of areas, including math, English composition, communication, science, and the humanities. Your college catalog should have valuable information regarding the G.E. courses you must take to complete your degree or program. Academic counselors can also show you how to make the most of the courses you select (e.g., whether you can fulfill more than one area, such as G.E. *and* major or graduation requirements with the same course).

FAQ: Why do I have to take General Education classes when I'm an Engineering/ Business/Political Science *(fill in the blank...)* major?

Let's face it- many students would never choose to take a math or literature or history class unless they were required to do so. But imagine a world where engineers never had to take a writing class... How would they convey their ideas to others in written form? Or what about a world where Liberal Arts majors never had to study math... How would they interpret statistical  reports? General Education requirements ensure that students have a well-rounded college curriculum. Instead of viewing G.E. and Graduation Requirements in a negative light, as many students do, try thinking of these as a chance to study subjects you normally wouldn't take. Who knows? As a result of taking G.E. classes, you may realize that you have a knack for History or Public Speaking or Astronomy. Studying General Education courses early in your college career can expose you to different fields of study. This can be especially helpful if you are undecided about a major. Exposure to different subjects may help you to realize that Political Science, or Math or Economics is definitely your field--- or perhaps definitely not your field!

General Education Exercise

To get the most out of your required General Education courses, complete the following steps:

1) List the major you plan to complete. If you are starting out at a community college and plan to transfer to a university, list the majors you will pursue at your community college *and* university.

2) Review your college catalog for the General Education requirements you will have to complete in order to graduate. You will most likely have to complete some G.E. courses in English Composition, Math, Science, and Humanities.

3) Identify all the classes that you could take to fulfill each specific requirement or area.

4) If you are enrolled in a community college and plan to earn a two year degree prior to transferring to a university to earn a four year degree, check to see which General Education courses will double-count (i.e., fulfill G.E. requirements at both campuses). Consult formal articulation agreements to verify transferability of course credit and check with your Academic Counselor for clarification or additional information, if needed.

5) Select your first choice for each G.E. category or area. Why did you select each particular course? What aspect(s) of these courses appeal to you?

6) List the career choice(s) you are considering.

7) List the types of skills (related to your career choice) you could develop as a result of taking each specific G.E. course. For example, someone pursuing a Business major with a concentration in Human Resources (and who eventually wants to be a corporate trainer) might select courses in Public Speaking, Psychology, or a foreign language to fulfill their G.E. requirements. Each of these courses could provide valuable skills for a future corporate trainer; corporate trainers will have to do extensive public speaking, they will want to have a clear understanding of human behavior, and they will expand their earning potential if they are able to speak more than one language.

8) Refer to the "What I Wish I'd Known In College" interview you conducted (see Chapter 5). Did the person you interviewed state that they wished they had taken courses other than what they selected? If yes, what type of courses did they say they wish they had taken? What were the reasons they wish they had taken these specific courses?

9) List your second choice of a course for each G.E. category (in case you can't get into your first choice class). What types of skills (related to your career choice) can you learn as a result of taking these courses?

Case Study: They Just Don't Understand Me

Carol had hated high school. She couldn't wait to go to college. In high school, she felt she was told where to go, what to do, and how to do it on a daily basis. In high school she was forced to study subjects she didn't want to study, that seemed to have no relevance to her life or her interests. She spent hours doodling in class to pass the time, and thinking about one day starting her own Interior Design business. Sometimes she would sketch elaborate designs for fabrics. Periodically she'd go through her notebooks and cut out her sketches, adding them to a binder of her drawings she had started years before. She complained to her parents and friends that the teachers didn't understand her and weren't really fair in their grading. She wanted the freedom to explore new subjects and felt stifled by the all the "ridiculous" requirements she had to meet to earn a high school diploma. She longed for the freedom of college, where she knew she would be able to pick her own classes and set her own schedule. Carol decided not to participate in her high school graduation ceremony. "Why bother?" she thought. "I don't have anything to celebrate. High school was torture and I'm just glad it's over. Now I can get on with my real life."

Carol was really looking forward to the start of Fall Semester classes at her new college. Since she was thinking about majoring in Art, she signed up to take Introduction to Photography and Art History. She had been surprised when she met with an Academic Advisor and was informed that, based on her assessment test scores, she would have to take a remedial writing class as part of her Fall Semester course load. She had always done well in her high school English classes and couldn't understand why she had to take a class that wouldn't even count towards her college degree. She was also shocked to find out that she would be required to complete three math courses, including Statistics in order to complete a Bachelor's degree. "I hate math!" she thought. "I can't believe they're going to make me take more of it in college. I mean, it's not like I want to be an engineer or anything. All I want to do is have my own Interior Design shop. I'm not going to need any math for that!"

The first few weeks of the semester passed quickly, and Carol fell into a routine of attending class and doing homework. While she loved her photography class, she felt bored in all her other classes; she found herself doodling while the professors droned on about certain artists or elaborated on proper sentence structure. Carol came down with colds and flu's three times during Fall Semester, and she ended up missing several classes. When her English papers came back with a C average, she began to feel like she was back in high school again. "My professor just doesn't understand me!" she said. "She tells us to interpret essays, and then dings me for how I interpret them. I don't think she really cares about what I think. She just wants me to tell her what she wants to hear." Towards the end of the semester, Carol's grandmother became seriously ill. Carol was very close to her and worried that she might lose her. She began having sleep problems, which made her unable to focus during lectures. Carol was relieved at the end of the semester when she had a break and was able to spend more time with her grandmother. She had decided to not take any more math or English classes for a while, and focus on her Art major instead. For Spring Semester she registered for three Art classes and one foreign language class, which she really didn't want to take, but was told by her Advisor was a requirement for graduation. During the winter break she thought about how the next semester would be so much better. She would finally be free to study what she loved. She put aside all thoughts of taking boring required courses and spent hours mentally designing the business she would one day own.

1)   Describe Carol's approach to learning.

2)   What are some unexpected challenges Carol faced during her first semester?

3)   How can Carol successfully achieve her long-term goals?

4)   List the ways Carol might be required to use math in her career as the owner of an Interior Design shop.

5)   What advice would you give to Carol about fulfilling courses such as General Education or graduation requirements?

Self-Assessment

Rate yourself on the behaviors of successful students on a scale of 1 – 5. How well prepared are you in the following areas?

    1 = I need lots of help with this

    2 = I could do better in this area

    3 = I'm OK in this area

    4 = I do a good job in this area

    5 = I'm very good at this

STUDY SKILLS

    ____   I know how to take good notes during lectures

    ____   I understand how to approach reading a large textbook

    ____   I know how to write effective essays and research papers

    ____   I limit my work hours at outside jobs so I can focus on school

    ____   I visit professors during their office hours

    ____   I know how to prepare for upcoming tests

    ____   I start preparing well before the date of my exams

    ____   I know how to run effective study groups

    ____   I understand what constitutes plagiarism and I know how to maintain academic integrity

Place a checkmark next to any items that you rated a 1 (I need lots of help with this) or a 2 (I could do better in this area). Identify where you could go to learn more about these areas.

Check your college's website or campus kiosks and bulletin boards for fliers announcing upcoming workshops on topics such as Effective Notetaking, Dealing With Test Anxiety, and How To Run Study Groups.

Stop by the Library to inquire about online tutorials or resource materials to help you properly cite sources when writing papers and how to research papers.

Chapter Notes: _____

Things to think about...

Things to remember...

Things to do....

Chapter 9

Keep On Winning

"Critical thinking is thinking about your thinking, while you're thinking, in order to make your thinking better."

Richard Paul

"We know that the average American, because of changes in the economy at home and abroad, will change work seven or eight times in a lifetime... If that is true, it is clear that we need an agenda as a people for a lifetime of learning."

Bill Clinton

"The best way to become an expert problem solver is to solve lots of problems."

Diane F. Halpern

Improving Your Critical Thinking Skills

You will be faced with *many* choices throughout life. These choices can be simple, such as, "Which coffeemaker (or cell phone or computer) should you buy?" or can be more complex and have a greater impact on your life, such as "Which career should you choose?" or "Should you get married and have children?" You will also have to solve many problems in college and throughout your career, such as figuring out how to get along with roommates or how to pay for your education, determining how to motivate others to achieve study or work goals, and developing new products or procedures to meet the needs of the changing workplace or market. Luckily, in college you get to spend years *learning how to learn.* While you won't learn the answers to all of life's questions in college, what you will gain (besides the knowledge specific to your major or career choice) are valuable, transferable skills you can use to approach problems and to make sound decisions throughout your career and life. Now is a great time to practice these skills (before you are faced with a huge task in your career where making a mistake could cost you your job, or your company thousands of dollars). As you face each new situation or solve each problem in college, you will utilize and further develop the very skills that can take you far in your career, such as the ability to communicate effectively, to use resources wisely, and to work well in teams. These skills, often referred to as "Soft Skills," are valued by employers and can set you apart from your colleagues early in your career and propel you to greater responsibility and positions of leadership. Soft skills are timeless (they are valuable and needed in every generation of workers) and can be applied over a series of jobs you may hold throughout your life and career.

While in college you'll probably hear the term "critical thinking skills" come up frequently. Although your professors might not directly state this in their syllabus or in class, they are working to help you to become better at critical thinking. You may be wondering, "What is critical thinking and why is it so important?" The best answer to this may be to think about what your life would be like without critical thinking skills. Imagine elections are coming up soon and one candidate promises to end the national deficit and put a million dollars in the pocket of each U.S. citizen. Would you vote for her? Perhaps you need to buy a car. You pull into the first car lot you see and the car salesman says that he has a car for sale that doesn't use gasoline, but instead runs off of plain water. Will you sign the contract? What if you need money for college and you are offered a job in a faraway country, with the promise that you can take all your classes online and finish your degree faster than if you stayed at your current college? Would you pack your bags? The critical thinking skills you develop in college can help you to confidently face situations, such as these, where there is a problem to be solved or a decision to be made, and know how best to proceed.

If critical thinking skills weren't all that difficult to acquire, you could probably skip college and just go to the bookstore and buy a book entitled "All The Answers You Will Ever Need In Life." However life isn't that easy and you will likely face many situations in college and in your career where you will need critical thinking skills.

- Is it better to finish college quickly even if it means taking on student loan debt, or is it better to take longer to complete your degree (so you can work more hours at an outside job to pay for college), yet graduate debt-free?

- Should you buy all new textbooks each semester, or save money by purchasing used textbooks or renting online texts?

- Should you major in Social Science, Dairy Science or Biological Science? Should you do a double major, or a major and a minor?

- Should you learn a new language or travel abroad as part of your college education? What if studying abroad means you end up adding an extra semester or year to your college curriculum? Is it worth taking longer to graduate and delaying entrance into the fulltime workforce so that you can experience living and studying in a different country?

- Once you graduate from college, is it better to earn less money in a job that you love, or to earn more money in a job that doesn't really appeal to you?

- What if you are offered a job promotion that will supercharge your career, but moving means uprooting your family from schools and a community they love?

These are just some examples of how you will need critical thinking skills throughout your life and career. Critical thinking skills allow you to think through a problem, situation or opportunity clearly and thoroughly, examine it from all angles and really understand the details and your options.

Fortunately, you have been using critical thinking skills most of your life. When you decided to go out for sports in high school or run for student government, you probably did not flip a coin to decide which sport or leadership position you chose, but you relied on critical thinking. When you decided which summer job or internship would pay the most (and be the most fun), and how to spend your summer earnings, you relied on critical thinking skills you had developed based on your previous experience earning and spending money. When you decided to date someone exclusively, or broke up with your boyfriend or girlfriend and chose to take a break from dating for a while, you most likely put a lot of thought into your decision. When you decided which colleges to apply to, and finally which one to attend, you probably took many things into consideration, from the reputation of the college, to the cost, to proximity to your home. It's important is to recognize that CRITICAL THINKING is not some big onerous skill that will take you years to master, but something that you have been practicing most of your life, and are constantly getting better at doing. College provides you years to practice creative problem solving and the art of decision making- the nuts and bolts of critical thinking.

So what does critical thinking entail, and how can you go about doing it effectively? In the book Learning To Think things Through Gerald M. Nosich notes, "Critical thinking is different from just thinking. It is metacognitive – it involves thinking about your thinking." He states that critical thinking involves 1) asking questions, 2) trying to answer those questions by reasoning them out, and 3) believing the results of (your) reasoning. In college you will have many opportunities to stop reading, studying, or going at full speed, and ask questions that enable you to reflect on how well you did (a metacognitive process). These opportunities for self-reflection occur at regular intervals between semesters or quarters, or school years (e.g., during summer break). Whether you aced all your classes or struggled through them this past term, it pays to focus on what worked (e.g., joining that study group or going to the Tutoring Center), which behaviors you should continue (e.g., doing the assigned reading before each lecture or class session), and what you need to do differently next term, if anything, so you can do better.

You could, of course, jump headfirst into each task without taking the time to think through how you want to proceed, in order to just finish them as quickly as possible. You could also take advice from the first person you see on how to proceed, do what you've always done, ignore information that is available, or do the first thing that "comes into your head." However, taking the time to think through and develop a strategy makes sense whether you are selecting your major, conducting a research project or about to plan a fundraiser for a student organization. Before you start studying for a test, or writing a long research paper, or determining the goals for an organization (or your future), take some time to think about how you want to proceed. Ask yourself the following questions:

- What is the best way to start?
- What information do I need before I can begin?
- How are others approaching this assignment/task?
- Am I clear about what it is I am trying to accomplish?
- What is the payoff in college or in my career for doing well on this task?

You might be thinking, "I don't really need to develop critical thinking skills--- anything I need to know I can just look up on the Internet." However, while the Internet brings vast resources to our fingertips, that information still "has to be selected, interpreted, digested, learned, and applied, or it is of no more use" than a huge library full of books that just sit on the shelves (Halpern, Chapter 1).

A college curriculum that helps you to develop critical thinking skills will require more of you than just memorizing information and regurgitating it on tests. Truly learning material means being able to do something with those facts, such as analyzing the information and applying the learnings to other settings or scenarios.

An example of a task that does *not* require much critical thinking would be the following:

> Memorize the names of all the Presidents of the United States.

A task that *does* involve critical thinking might look more like this:

> Select the three U.S. Presidents you believe were the most effective. Elaborate on their accomplishments and compare them with the three U.S. Presidents you believe were the least effective in their jobs. Justify why you selected your three top presidents.

While you might be able to memorize the names of all the U.S. Presidents for a test, you will likely forget those names as soon as the test is over. However, if you spend hours researching and thinking about the U.S. Presidents to complete the more comprehensive assignment, you will utilize more complex critical thinking skills, and will be more likely to remember what you learned long after the assignment is completed. As you move from introductory courses in your major to more specific courses, you will be required to complete and solve increasingly complex levels of tasks and problems to demonstrate your understanding of the material. If you pursue a graduate degree after completing your undergraduate degree, you will have even more opportunities to take what you are learning to greater depths and further develop your critical thinking skills.

Critical Thinking Example

Your professor asks you to demonstrate your ability to think critically by writing a 10 page essay about a movie you have seen recently. Your instructions are to give an overview of the movie, show that you understand the main points, outline how you can apply the learnings from the movie to your life, analyze the parts of the movie and make some generalizations to the world at large, synthesize different aspects or new themes for a sequel, and evaluate whether this movie is worth seeing by others. How would you begin?

You might start by sharing your general **knowledge** about the movie (#1 Give an overview of the movie):

- **Recall** the names of the actors or the main characters.
- **Where** does the story take place?
- **Describe** how the actors dressed in the movie.
- **How** did the characters interact with one another?
- **When** did the movie really get your attention?
- **List** three key scenes in the movie.

Next you might show your **comprehension** of the main themes in the movie (#2 Show that you understand the main points):

- **Outline** the main parts of the story.
- **Compare** the acting ability of the two main actors/actresses.
- **Contrast** the "good guy" versus "bad guy" in the movie.
- **Rephrase** the main point or motto of the movie in your own words.
- **Interpret** what the main character meant when s/he said…
- **Summarize** the movie.

You then could show the **application** of the learnings to your own life (#3 Outline how you can apply the learnings from the movie to your life):

- **Apply** what you learned from the movie to a real life situation you are experiencing.

- **Develop** the plot for a sequel to the movie.

- **Give examples** of how the movie kept your attention.

- If you could **change one thing** about the movie, what would it be and why?

- Which character do you **identify** with the most?

Next, you could give a more detailed **analysis** of the movie (#4 Analyze the parts of the movie and make some generalizations to the world at large):

- **Examine** each of the characters and describe the **relationship** between them.

- **Survey** others to see what they thought about the movie.

- **Simplify** the main point of the movie to one sentence.

- **Explain why** you think the director chose the main actors.

- Outline some **conclusions** you think the writer of the movie wanted the audience to believe about life on a broader level.

- What was the **function** of the supporting actors?

Then you could **synthesize** information to propose alternate outcomes in the movie (#5 Synthesize different aspects or new themes for a sequel):

- **Change** the setting of the movie to 100 years earlier.

- **Modify** the story by changing the scenery.

- **Improve** the movie by **developing** your own ending.

- Could you **predict** how well a sequel to this movie would do?

- Think of a new **original** title for the movie.

- How would you **estimate** the audience's willingness to watch a sequel to this movie?

And finally you could conduct an **evaluation** of the movie (#6 Evaluate whether this movie is worth seeing by others):

- **Evaluate** whether this was a good or bad movie.

- **Judge** the "Oscar-worthiness" of the main actors.

- **Who** would be your first choice to star in a remake of this movie?

- Would you **recommend** that your friends see this movie?

- **Justify** why it's worth your friends spending money to see the movie.

- **Rate** the movie on a scale of 1 – 10.

- **Explain** why it was better than other movies that are in the theatres right now.

(Based on Quick Flip questions for Critical Thinking by Linda G. Barton - based on the original Bloom's Taxonomy)

So if you've ever shared your thoughts or opinions about a movie you've seen with others, you have most likely utilized many different critical thinking skills. You can take this same critical thinking model (referred to as Bloom's Taxonomy of Learning) and use it to develop everything from plans for an upcoming party or social event (determining where the event will take place, deciding the theme, brainstorming ideas to make the event interesting, predicting what others will like, and finally evaluating the event), to the outline for a research paper (determining the facts, stating your thesis, developing examples to support your thesis, showing your understanding of the topic, and proposing new ideas and making recommendations). Start with sharing things you know about the topic, and move towards a more complex analysis and evaluation of the topic.

Effective Problem Solving

Welcome To The Rest Of Your Life...

As an undergraduate I was very involved in student activities. Since I was thinking of pursuing a career in Higher Education, I took advantage of many different opportunities to run student organizations and to develop my leadership skills. Once I ran into an administrator and mentioned to him that I was on my way to one of five meetings I had that day. He responded, "Get used to it. Your life will always be this way." Sure enough, I have sat through countless meetings in my different  jobs, and my schedule is always full. It's comforting to think that you may not always be as busy as you are in college- that the pace of your life will eventually slow down. However, if you are busy in college, you will probably be busy in life. College gives you the chance to learn how to manage your time well. Being able to juggle multiple responsibilities now, can help you to be good at multi-tasking later. Now is also a great time to develop the decision making and problem solving skills you will need to call upon repeatedly throughout your life and career.

Some people dread the idea of dealing with problems or having to make decisions. They worry that they won't know how to solve a problem, and about whether they're making the right decision. They may avoid problem situations or stall when it comes to having to decide, or even put off making decisions altogether. Should you upgrade your cell phone? Should you go to graduate school, or go to work after you finish your degree? Should you complete a work internship, or take your chances entering the job market without having any work experience in your field? Sometimes the clock or calendar forces you to decide (e.g., you must declare your academic major by a certain deadline). Sometimes others will decide for you, such as when a friend says "If I don't hear from you by Friday, I'll assume you don't want to hang out this weekend." Think of some decisions you have made in the past. How did you go about deciding what to do? How can you face making decisions comfortably and not resort to flipping a coin to figure out your next career move or other big decision? Thankfully, there are some easy tools you can use to help you break down problems so that you can ultimately make a decision.

Problem Solving Practice Exercise

You are trying to decide whether you should live in the campus dorms again next year, or rent an apartment off campus with a couple of friends. How can you analyze this situation to make a decision?

The Interaction Problem Solving Model (Doyle & Strauss) outlines a useful approach to problem solving in group settings. It consists of 6 parts, with most of your energy and attention going to the first three phases.

Phase #1   How do you perceive the problem?

Acknowledge your **emotions** around the issue.

> How do you feel about living in the dorms? How about your friends?

Try to zero in on the **real problem**.

> Has living in the dorms been problematic? Is there anything you didn't like about living in the dorms that is making you consider moving off campus?

Ask "What's the **best/worst/most probable outcome** if we address this problem?"

> What's the worst thing that could happen if you stayed in the dorms another year? What's the best thing that could happen? Ask the same questions about living off campus.

Ask **"Whose problem is it?"**

> Perhaps you really like living in the dorms, but your friends don't.

Phase #2   Define the problem

State the **problem as a question**

"Should I move off campus next year and rent an apartment with my friends?"

Try to **group similar ideas together** ("lasso" them)

Could you and your friends move to a different dorm together, or is an apartment your only chance to live together? Is this an either/or situation? Can you do both X *and* Y?

Make a list of what you know **the problem is/is not**

The problem is:

Living in the dorms *is* very expensive.

Students living in the dorms are forced to purchase an expensive meal plan.

Students living in the dorms can't cook their own food.

The dorms tend to be full of younger students who are more interested in social events than in studying.

The problem is not:

It is not an issue of living close to the center of campus (as apartments are available to rent right next to the campus).

It is not an issue of not liking your dorm-mates (you get along well with the other students living in the dorm).

It is not an issue of the dorms being run down (they were recently renovated).

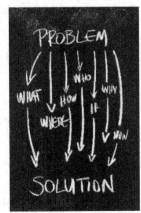

Diagram - can you make a **visual representation** of it?

Phase #3   Analyze the problem

<u>Ask basic questions (**who, what, when, where, why, how**?)</u>

Who is involved in making this decision?

What are you looking for in a living situation?

By when do you have to make a decision about next year's living arrangements?

Where are the off-campus apartments located?

Why have you been thinking about moving off campus?

How will you go about making a decision? How will you handle the logistics of moving?

<u>Break the problem down</u> <u>into smaller parts or different issues.</u>

Are finances pushing you to find a more economical living situation?

Is it too noisy in the dorms to study?

Are you forced to share a room with someone you do not choose when living in the dorms?

<u>Conduct a **force field analysis**: Ask *What are all the things contributing to the problem? **What are all the things keeping the problem from getting worse?)</u>

*The price of living in the dorms goes up every year.

*The campus Housing Policies do not allow you to choose your own roommate in the dorms.

*You do not get to decide who else lives in the dorm.

**You know what it is like living in the dorms (and you've survived).

**You know what the cafeteria food tastes like (and you've survived).

Ask the experts on the subject for their opinions.

> Talk to others who have moved off campus after living in the dorms. Ask them what they liked/didn't like about living in an apartment. If they had to decide all over again, would they still make the same decision?

Spend about 80% of your time on the first three phases of this problem solving model. The better you understand the problem or the decision to be made, the easier it will be to come up with possible solutions.

Phase #4   Spend some time generating alternatives

Quickly **brainstorm** as many possible solutions as you can.

Think of as many options for your living arrangements as quickly as possible, without stopping to decide if they are feasible, or good or bad options.

Think about **how others have dealt with this situation** before.

Perhaps you know of others who rented a house instead of an apartment together, and that worked out better for them than renting an apartment.

Write all your ideas down on Post-It notes or index cards, **then physically move them around** to try to see things in a different perspective.

Phase #5   Begin to evaluate your different options

<u>**Develop a grid (a criteria checkerboard)**</u> where you list your options on the left, and the criteria you want to meet on the top.

✔	Comfortable living environment	Cost effective	Close enough to ride a bike to classes	Can live with friends
Living in the dorms				
Moving to a different dorm				
Moving to an apartment				
Moving into a house				

<u>**Rank your options by order of preference**</u> (the first one is your first choice, the second is your second choice, and so on).

See if you can sort the options into different categories.

List the advantages and disadvantages of each option or proposed solution.

Ask everyone involved what they think about each possible solution and why they like each alternative.

Phase #6   Make your decision

Try to reach a **decision by consensus** that everyone can support (as opposed to deciding by a "majority rules" vote).

> Make sure everyone involved can live with the final solution.

See if you can **combine more than one solution**.

> Perhaps you can move into off campus (private) dorms that allow more flexibility in choosing meal plans.

Add or subtract from the different options to see if that makes any of them more agreeable.

Take a quick vote to see if everyone involved in making the decision is thinking alike (which will save you time in debating the pros and cons of each option).

Ask everyone to **vote on which options they want to eliminate**.

> Perhaps everyone is in agreement that they don't want to rent a house. Take things that everyone does not want off the table.

If you get bogged down in the decision making process, **go back to your original goals, or review how you agreed to make a final decision**.

Remember what you are looking for in a new living arrangement. Review any agreements you made early on in the decision making process.

If necessary, **go back to the first phases of this problem solving model and repeat** any steps that could be helpful.

Obtain feedback. How did it work out? What do you need to change to improve your decision making process next time?

> If you need to find housing for 4 or more years while in college, you can use this problem solving model to review what worked well at the end of each year, and decide if there's anything you want to change about your living situation.

Problem Solving Strategies

The authors of this problem solving and decision making method suggest keeping track of the strategies you try, then considering other strategies if you or the group you are in gets stuck trying to make a decision.

The following is an adapted list from their Strategy Notebook:

Adapt your ideas

Assume that any of your options will work

Build up ideas (add to them)

Check the details

Combine one or more options

Commit to doing something

Compare your answers with others

Copy what others have done

Defer to the experts

Draw a diagram

Decide what each option means

Define what success looks like

Dream about the possibilities

Expand on some of your ideas

Eliminate options you know won't work

Focus on the end product

Generalize about this problem to other similar problems

Guess which option is best

Hold back on taking action

Hypothesize what would happen if...

Imagine success

Leap in and just try something

Memorize your options

Organize your options into groups or different classifications

Plan the details

Post your options on a wall chart

Predict what will happen

Purge things that don't work

Question who/what/why/where/how

Recall previous similar situations

Record your options or information

Reduce the total number of options you have

Relate this issue to others

Repeat what works

Search available resources

Select one of your options

Separate out different parts

Substitute one item for another

Test your options to see which ones would work

Translate the information into other terms

Vary your responses

Set up a **visual display**

Visualize the end product

Think of a problem you are facing or a decision that you have to make, and work through the different steps of this problem solving model to see if you can find a solution. You do not need to use every single tool in each phase of the model. Pick and choose the tools that you prefer or that work best with this particular situation.

Phase #1   How do you perceive the problem?

Phase #2   Define the problem

Phase #3   Analyze the problem

Phase #4   Spend some time generating alternatives

Phase #5   Begin to evaluate your different options

Phase #6   Make your decision

Creative Problem Solving

101 Jobs

Brainstorming is a very effective critical thinking tool that can be used when solving problems or making decisions. Essentially, you come up with as many ideas or possible solutions to a problem as quickly as possible, without stopping to evaluate the ideas or determine if they are feasible.

I recently worked with a group of high school seniors and gave them the following scenario:

You have 20 minutes to think of 100 jobs you could do to help pay your way through college.

I issued them this challenge to help them to understand that while college *is* expensive, they have numerous ways to earn money while attending school and during summer breaks (and therefore, the lack of money or "not having enough money" would be eliminated in their mind as a reason why they could not achieve a college degree). I broke the students into three teams, and they competed to see which group could come up with the most ideas for types of jobs or places to work. Sure enough, at the end of 20 minutes, the students had brainstormed over 100 ways to earn money to pay for college- everything from starting a dog-walking service, to house-sitting (see partial list on the next page). How many solutions could you think of for a problem you are facing if you really freed yourself up to creatively brainstorm?

Try this exercise with a couple of friends and see what you can come up with in 10 minutes:

- 50 names for a rock band

- 50 themes for a dorm party

- 50 ways to save money in college

- 50 ideas for promoting college success

You'll probably be surprised at not only the number of ideas you come up with, but the number of ideas that come up synergistically (i.e., as a result of all of you putting your heads together). Practicing critical thinking skills such as creative problem solving can give you great confidence in approaching tasks you will face throughout your career and in your life.

Almost 100 Ways To Earn Money For College

Apply for scholarships	Arcade Worker
Artist (sell your creations)	Athletic Events Security Guard
Babysitting	Bake Sales
Bartender	Bookkeeper
Bus Driver	Burger Flipper
Bus Tables	Buy & Sell Stocks
Candle Maker	Car Washer
Carpool Driver	Cashier
Catering	Chef
Cleaning Houses	Coach Little League
Construction Worker (seasonal)	Cook
Cosmetologist (Hair Stylist)	Custodian
Dance Instructor	Dishwasher
Dog Walker	Drink Runner
Editor	Enter contests (for cash prizes)
Enter pageants	Fact Checker
Factory Worker	Fast Food Worker
Farmer (grow organic food)	Federal Workstudy Employee
Field Worker	Food Stand Operator
Fork Lift Driver	Fundraisers (raffles)
Garage Sales / Yard Sales	Gardener
Gas Station Attendant	Hostess (Restaurant)
Ice Cream Scooper	Internships
Juice Bar Smoothie Maker	Janitor
Journalist	Law Firm (Legal Clerk)
Lawn Mower	Lemonade Stand
Life Guard	Magazine Seller
Mechanic	Military
Model	Newspaper Deliverer
Note Taker	Painter (houses)
Park Ranger	Patent ideas (Inventor)
Photographer	Physical Trainer
Pizza Maker	Pool Cleaner
Postal Worker	Proof Reader
Receptionist – Doctor's Office	Recycle cans
Referee	Research Subject (clinical trials)
Retail Sales	Sandwich Maker
School Crossing Guard	Seasonal Worker
Secretary	Sell stuff on Ebay
Sign Twirler	Special Education Aide
Starbucks Barista	Telemarketer
Theater Ticket Taker	Theme Park Attendant
Tow Truck Driver	Trash Collector
Tutor	Valet
Waiter / Waitress	Warehouse Worker
Welder	Yard Maintenance
Yogurt Shop	Zoo Cage Cleaner

Chapter Notes:

Things to think about...

Things to remember...

Things to do....

Chapter 10

Making The Most Of
Your College Experience

"Preservation of one's own culture does not require contempt or disrespect for other cultures."

Cesar Chavez

"Universities and colleges offer unequaled opportunities for students to meet others who are different from themselves and to enter into dialogue with them... International students, students from different religions and cultures, students who share your goals in education but may differ from you in almost every other way- these are people worth seeking out, for they can teach you about themselves and about yourself."

Virginia N. Gordon and Thomas L. Minnick

Multicultural Perspectives On College And Career

College offers you the chance to learn and grow in numerous ways. The day you cross the stage to receive your diploma, you'll want to know that you took advantage of the variety of learning experiences across campus. This includes having taken advantage of the many opportunities to interact with others from different backgrounds.

Think about the college or university you are attending- in what ways are the students and faculty diverse? How do you think the campus diversity (or perhaps the lack thereof) influences the learning environment? Perhaps college has provided you the opportunity to move across the country, or to interact with others who are very different than students from your high school, or people from your neighborhood or town. However, even if you are attending your local college, you are sure to encounter students from all over the world (such as International Students) that can add to your college experience, and help you to learn to work successfully in a diverse workforce.

To find out more about the diversity of your campus, check you college's website for statistics about the student population and faculty. You can also learn more about the diversity of your campus by stopping by your college's Associated Students or Student Activities Office, or by visiting the Multicultural Center, as well as by participating in events designed to provide a supportive environment for different groups of people based on their interests or backgrounds. Some colleges have ethnic theme house dorms where the language, food and customs of different cultures are emphasized. Taking a Foreign Language course or participating in a Study Abroad Program (where you take college courses in another country) are also great ways to prepare for any career you choose. Even spending time at the campus coffee house, asking other students about their life experiences and individual backgrounds, can enrich your overall college experience and help you to gain the skills you need to work in a global economy. Seek out opportunities to meet students from other dorms or parts of campus who can add to your overall educational experience because of their own cultural or ethnic background. This can be done through informal meals at ethnic theme houses or dorms, by attending cultural performances on campus, or even by attending the meetings of different student organizations on campus.

Exercise:

Think for a minute about something that represents your cultural or ethnic background, or something that reflects your unique upbringing. Take a plain piece of paper and draw something that symbolizes this (e.g., you might draw a food specific to your culture or a picture of a custom that is part of your background).

Journal Assignment:

Spend 20 minutes writing about the picture you drew, and how it represents your culture or background. Elaborate on what aspects of your culture or background you would be willing to share with other students. Note what you would like to learn about students from other backgrounds while you are in college, and list some specific steps to achieve these goals.

"It is difficult to imagine the tremendous effect that culture has on the way we think without an extended experience in a culture other than the one you know best. It is for this reason that I tout the benefits of extended foreign travel. It can change your worldview..."

Diane F. Halpern

Opportunities For Multicultural Education

Here are some ways to make the most of the multicultural learning environment available at your college or university:

- Meet people from all over the world by seeking out students who have immigrated or who are International Students. These may become life-long friendships, affording you the opportunity to someday visit your friends in other countries, or even build on their global professional networks for future job opportunities.

- Participating in a Study Abroad Program may be an option for you, regardless of your major. Stop by your campus Study Abroad or Overseas Studies Office early in your freshman year to find out what opportunities are available to you, and how these could fit into or complement your major. If your college has a Foreign Language Proficiency Requirement for graduation, studying in another country for a semester or summer session may help you to fulfill this.

  Note: Some Study Abroad programs will require you to be proficient in another language at the 2nd year college level in order to participate, as courses are taught in that language. There may be programs offered in other countries where English is the dominant language, or in countries where the courses are taught in English although another language is spoken. This is an option for students who wish to study abroad, but do not have the time to become fluent in a second language prior to beginning their program.

- You can attend cultural fairs or festivals held on campus to learn about and try different foods, music and customs.

- Many campuses have different cultural centers or a multicultural center that serve as the hub of student activity for ethnic events on campus.

- You can venture off campus to participate in cultural events specific to the area where you are attending college. Check out restaurants that highlight the food of local ethnic groups.

- You can practice your foreign language skills by interacting with others who are from the country where the language you are learning is spoken.

- Multicultural course or foreign language course graduation requirements provide excellent opportunities to learn about the culture of other groups, or to try a course such as Cross Cultural Communication, ethnic history, or International Business.

- You can better prepare to work in an increasingly global community by attending campus workshops or listening to guest speakers from different countries.

Be sure to set some learning goals related to interacting with people from different cultural and ethnic backgrounds early on in your college career! This will be helpful when you apply for jobs and you are asked by a potential employer to give examples of your ability to work with people who are different from you. Being able to work successfully in a diverse environment will make you more marketable after graduation and throughout your career, no matter which field you enter.

Appreciating Diversity

Answer the following questions:

Do you feel you "fit in" at your college or university? If yes, elaborate. If no, why not?

Since enrolling in college have you interacted with 2 or more people who are very different from you?

If yes, what have you learned as a result of interacting with them?

If no, what could you do to increase the likelihood that you will meet and interact with others in college who are different from you?

Do you celebrate holidays or special occasions with special food, music or customs based on your background or ethnic/cultural upbringing? If yes, please elaborate.

Have you had the opportunity to share customs or traditions related to your culture or your unique personal background with others at your campus? If yes, give an example.

Can you think of some opportunities you may have while in college to share your culture or unique background with others?

Describe a positive trait, characteristic or value that you have as result of your upbringing or your cultural background:

Do you think you will carry this trait/characteristic/value with you when you leave college and enter the workforce? If yes, how do you think this trait/characteristic/value will influence your behavior in the workplace?

What positive contribution can you make to the campus and future work environment as a result of your cultural background or own unique upbringing (e.g., values, beliefs, traditions, food, music, religion, approaches to working with others)?

Have you considered taking any courses which emphasize the ethnic/cultural experience of a particular group? If so, elaborate.

Have you considered studying abroad (e.g., overseas) as part of your college education?

If yes, where would you consider studying? What do you think you could learn as a result of studying abroad that could help you in your career?

If no, describe some other ways you could increase your knowledge and understanding of other cultures that could be beneficial once you enter your professional career:

Do you think the lessons you learn while in college about how to work better with others who are different from you will benefit you later in life? If yes, elaborate

Myth #10 - Activities outside of attending class or studying are a waste of time.

Employers are looking for college graduates that not only have a degree and/or special training, but also have strong critical thinking and creative problem solving skills, good interpersonal skills, common sense, and the ability to work well in groups and to lead others. Many of these skills don't come from sitting in a classroom, but develop when you interact with other students in work and social situations. At one university where I worked, there were more than 350 student organizations for a student body of 16,000. That averaged out to one club for every 45 students on campus! Employers are looking for college graduates with leadership skills and potential. The best place to develop these skills is through work experience, and by interacting with others in student clubs and organizations. When you go out to apply for jobs, It never hurts to be able to say "I was the President of the Entrepreneurs Club at my university," or "I oversaw the annual canned food drive on our campus, and under my leadership we doubled the amount of donations received in just two years." That is the kind of information that is sure to catch employers' attention. Make the most of your college years by getting involved in student clubs and by completing at least one internship related to your career.

Get Involved! Opportunities For Leadership Development

College provides many opportunities to become involved in extracurricular activities. There are numerous pre-professional, special interest, and social clubs and organizations on most college campuses. Getting involved in campus clubs can help you to develop the marketable skills that employers seek in new hires and that will make you more competitive in the job market, such as effective communication, creative problem solving, decision making, and the ability to work well in groups. Taking on a leadership role in campus organizations can also enhance your overall classroom experience, and give you the opportunity to practice the skills that will be required of you in the world of work as a future supervisor, trainer, or project manager.

Here are some other benefits of getting involved in activities outside of your college classes:

- You will get to meet students outside of your dorm or immediate social circle.

- You can socialize with others who share common interests.

- You can learn how to run effective meetings and use Parliamentary Procedure.

- You can dedicate time and energy to issues or causes that interest you (such as conservation, politics, or community service).

- You can contribute to the overall campus life and strengthen your learning community.

- You can join a pre-professional organization related to your major or career, and start networking and making valuable contacts you can tap once you enter the job market.

- You will have the opportunity to mentor other students.

- You can become skilled at event planning.

- You can learn more about a new area that interests you.

- You can take on a supporting role that builds on your strengths and talents, such as fundraising, marketing, web resources, writing or record keeping.

- You will have the opportunity to interact with faculty club advisors who can serve as references for you when you apply to graduate school, or for summer or fulltime jobs.

To learn more about opportunities for extracurricular involvement at your college or university, stop by the Associated Students Government Office or your campus Office of Student Activities. Be strategic about selecting which clubs you will join; consider the overall learning goals you listed in Chapter 1. What do you want to learn while in college besides the academic material you will study? Student clubs can round out your learning experience, and help you to find the right balance of work, personal development, and play while in college.

Extracurricular Involvement

Answer the following questions:

How many student organizations exist on your college or university campus?

List three clubs you would consider joining while in college.

What about these organizations interests you?

Do you consider yourself a leader?

      If yes, elaborate.

      If no, what would need to happen for you to take on a leadership role?

What leadership positions have you held prior to enrolling in college?

What skills could you contribute to a student organization?

Is there a student club that you wish existed on your college campus?

Would you be willing to start this new club on campus?

List some college courses that would help you to strengthen your skills as a leader:

List some college courses that would strengthen your ability to work well in groups:

"The Reluctant Leader"

At some point in your life, you may find you have become a leader. You won't decide to be a leader, you won't ask to be a leader, but you will become one anyway- albeit reluctantly. It could be that you are quite content to not lead anyone anywhere. You won't necessarily even see yourself as possessing leadership skills. Yet, as if some unknown forces are conspiring, you will be asked to take on a leadership role, or even more mysteriously, you will find yourself in a leadership position and wonder how you ever got there. Perhaps your classmates will nominate you to coordinate a charitable fundraising campaign, or a church official will ask you to start a youth group, or your neighbors will push you into overseeing a campaign to make the neighborhood safer by lowering the speed limit.

Before you know it, you are knee-deep in leadership tasks. You find yourself organizing a meeting, setting an agenda, or circulating a petition. You may assume these tasks, all the while believing that you are incapable of being successful at leading others- after all, you have never taken on a leadership role before. You'll remember that life was pretty good when you left the leadership tasks to others. Sometimes you followed. Sometimes you observed. Leadership was something others did. But now it is your turn.

People will point you out to others - "Go see Ted- he's in charge." Your cell phone will ring and individuals you have never met will offer advice, assistance, resources, and even unsolicited criticism. A newspaper reporter will contact you and ask for a quote for an article she is writing about volunteerism, or keeping kids out of trouble, or creating safer college campuses. You may find yourself worrying about being selected as a spokesperson for that specific issue. You are, after all, just a regular person. The only thing that set you apart, is that you said "yes," albeit reluctantly, when leadership came knocking on your door.

Eventually you may reach a point where you swear you'll never again allow yourself to be coerced into being placed in charge of a project. You'll wistfully think about all the things you will do when this "it" is over, this fundraiser, or club event, or political campaign. Your leadership task will be all-consuming. You will obsess over it, worry about the details, dream about it, and talk to others incessantly about IT. You will become angry with people who tell you you're doing it the wrong way, while they sit back and observe from the comfort of their non-leadership positions.

Yet, you will be surprised as others step up to the plate, pitch in, donate time or money, and help you to accomplish the task at hand or realize your vision for the way things must be. You will be grateful for small compliments, for the reassuring looks of authority figures, for the smiles on the faces of the people you have helped. You will marvel at how the myriad details seem to come together at just the right time and your task, your project, your event is pulled off with amazing success. You may even find that this leadership thing isn't so bad, after all. You'll find you *do* have opinions, and you *are* willing to take risks and venture into new areas. You may even find yourself waiting for your phone to ring so you can discuss the innumerable details and small triumphs with people you've never really interacted with before.

Once this leadership thing is over, you'll take a few days to relax, to savor the thrill of victory, and to focus on what you learned and how it all came together. You'll remind yourself of your promise not to take on any more leadership roles, because you are not a leader, and there is nothing really special about you anyway. Yet, just when everything seems to be settling down, those mysterious forces will once again beckon you. Your friends or classmates will raise wary eyebrows as if to say, "But you said...!" And you will find yourself once again, perhaps not quite so reluctantly, saying "yes" to leadership.

Journal Response

Have you ever been a reluctant leader? Do you prefer to be the leader or a follower in work groups? What traits or skills do you look for in a study group leader? Do you think you will be in a leadership (management, trainer, or supervisor) role in your career? What can you do while in college to strengthen your leadership skills?

Chapter Notes:

Things to think about...

Things to remember...

Things to do....

Chapter 11

Stay In the Game

"If we did everything we are capable of, we would astound ourselves."

Thomas A. Edison

Staying Healthy In College

Most students face at least a few obstacles to completing their degree. What are some things that could become obstacles to earning your college degree? When planning for your academic success, be sure to think about your overall physical and emotional health. How can you make sure that you don't burn out from exhaustion midway through the semester, or face a sexually transmitted disease or unplanned pregnancy, or develop a dependence on substances such as alcohol or drugs to get by? Most college campuses have a Health Center where students can go to get information about or assistance in staying healthy. Many college campuses also have a Counseling & Psychological Services Center that provides support to students who are experiencing crisis situations, such as feeling depressed due to the death of a loved one, or who are experiencing anxiety from the pressure of college life. How do you know when you should seek outside help for a problem you are experiencing?

When To See A Professional Counselor:

- You experience feelings of depression that persist more than a week or seem to come out of nowhere.

- You are having difficulty sleeping or are sleeping too much.

- You have frequent headaches or stomachaches you think might be stress-related.

- You are binge-eating or purging to lose weight, or you have lost your appetite or are over-eating to deal with stress.

- You are turning to alcohol or drugs to deal with pressure or to unwind.

- You have thoughts of taking your own life, or believe that your family and friends would be better off without you.

- You feel overwhelmed by a traumatic incident such as the death of someone close to you or some other great loss.

- You no longer feel joy or enthusiasm when doing activities you have always loved.

- A friend or your Academic Counselor suggests you would benefit by speaking to a professional mental health counselor.

Speaking with a professional counselor can help you to sort out what's really going on. Perhaps you're in the wrong major and that is a source of stress. Or you may be struggling with self-esteem issues. Or you're even dreading graduating from college because you don't know what's ahead of you. Many college campuses allow students to meet with a professional counselor for a few sessions at no cost to them (this service is covered by their student fees or their campus health insurance). You'll be amazed how much better you'll feel after sharing whatever is burdening you with a trained professional. Students who need more counseling sessions beyond what the campus health professionals can provide are generally referred out to community services or to private health practitioners covered by their own health insurance. Counselors can also refer students to doctors or nurse practitioners in the Campus Health Center for needed medications or health screenings.

Look up the following information so that you have it handy, if needed:

- What is the phone number of your college's Health Center? _____

- What is the phone number of your college's Counseling & Psychological Services Center? _____

- What is the name and phone number of a trusted friend or family member you can call if you are feeling stressed or overwhelmed in college? _____ _____

Staying physically active is an important part of staying healthy and succeeding in college. If you don't feel well, it will be hard to put in the long hours needed to study and complete assignments. With some advance thought, you can build regular exercise into your daily routine without necessarily committing to working out at a gym- this can save you time and money in the long run. Do you live on campus? Take the long way when walking to your classes. Take a brisk walk around the perimeter of the campus between classes or during your lunch break. Avoid driving and choose to ride your bicycle instead. If you live off campus, try walking or biking to campus instead of taking public transit. Take part in social activities such as weekend dances or intramural sports, and get your heart rate up. You'll have fun and burn extra calories while you're at it. Can you take P.E. classes to meet any of your degree requirements? Sign up for jazz dance, yoga, or try a class in the martial arts. Instead of texting your friends who live in the next dorm, run over there and see if you can catch them in their rooms. Take the stairs instead of the elevator. Meet a couple of friends for a walking break- you walk and talk at the same time. Aim for at least 30 minutes a day of walking at a brisk pace, jogging, biking, or some other type of exercise. Keeping your energy up will enable you to handle longer class and study sessions.

STAY IN THE GAME   219

How much time would you like to spend in physical activity per week?

My goal is to exercise _____ minutes daily, or _____ hours weekly.

> Note here how much time you spend walking to and from class and around campus daily:
>
> How much time do you spend biking daily (if applicable)?
>
> How much time do you spend per week in P.E. classes that have you actively moving (e.g., yoga, spinning, karate, etc.)?
>
> How much time do you spend in Intramural Sports each week?
>
> On average how much time do you spend per week dancing (attending dances in the dorms, formal events, or parties)?
>
> Are you involved in any cultural dance groups or other groups such as a Hiking Club where you get physical exercise? If so, how many hours per week do you spend in these activities?
>
> Are there any other activities where you get physical exercise (e.g., at your job or working out at a gym)? If so, how many hours per week do you spend doing this?

Add up the number of minutes and hours you spend doing each of these activities, as well as others to determine the average amount of time you spend moving or exercising per week.

> On average I spend _____ hours per week exercising.

Subtract the number of hours of physical activity you get from the number of hours you would like to exercise.

> The number of hours you stated you want to exercise each week _____
>
> Subtract the number of hours of exercise that you get each week _____
>
> = The amount of activity you must add to your weekly schedule to meet your goal _____

If you are not getting enough physical activity, brainstorm some ways you could add more movement and exercise into your daily, weekly and monthly routine.

If you are meeting or exceeding your weekly exercise goal, congratulate yourself and keep up the good work!

Another way to stay healthy in college is to follow your mother's advice: Wash your hands frequently, especially before eating or preparing food. Remember to get your flu shot! Stay home if you feel a cold or flu coming on. Take vitamins and remedies to ease any colds you get, and be sure to get lots of rest at the first sign of an illness. Pick healthy foods at the grocery store instead of

loading up on packaged noodles or heading out for fast food. Carry healthy snacks with you in your backpack so that you won't be tempted to buy junk food from vending machines. Don't burn the candle at both ends, i.e., make sure you are getting enough sleep. And never share food or drinks with others.

Many college students live in dorms where they are required to purchase a meal plan which can cost thousands of dollars. It can be tempting to try to get your money's worth when eating your meals in the cafeteria. Make a commitment to skip the soda machine. Stop by the salad bar and fill up on leafy green vegetables first, before heading for the entrée line. Skip dessert, or have fresh fruit for dessert. Plan health study breaks with your friends- instead of ordering in pizza at night (a sure way to pack on extra pounds), try low fat popcorn or veggie sticks,

or have everyone bring a different kind of fruit and whip up a quick fruit salad. Invest in a coffee maker, and make your own low fat coffee drinks, herbal teas, or hot chocolate (and skip the whipped cream). Your pocketbook will thank you later, and you won't have to wonder why your jeans are so tight come mid-semester!

Alcohol Awareness

Educating yourself about alcohol is another important step in staying healthy in college. As a new college student, you'll find that the first few weeks of school there are many parties being held in campus dorms, and in off campus houses, including fraternities and sororities. Alcohol and drugs can frequently be found, and in abundance. You may feel pressure to "do what everyone else is doing" simply because you think that's what everyone is doing!

College students often make the mistake of thinking that they are invincible. In the protected environment of the college campus, they may try risky behaviors they might not have done in the past, such as dating or hooking up with complete strangers, binge drinking, recreational drug use, leaning over the edge of a four story balcony at a party while intoxicated, or other assorted acts that, unfortunately, result in great bodily harm. When "everybody's doing it" (whatever *it* may be) and seemingly getting away with it, they believe "Bad things only happen to other people - nothing bad can happen to me!" While many years have passed since I was a college student, I clearly remember the sense that so many of my classmates had that they were invincible- the future was bright, they were privileged, attending a top university, and... nothing bad could or would ever happen to them (because bad things only happened to other people). Apparently, parents and administrators have worried for over 100 years that bad things could happen by sending their sons off to college (women were not found as frequently on college campuses in the past). In my office hangs a very old print dated 1878 entitled "College: The Road To Ruin." In it, a group of young men are seen playing cards, smoking, drinking in excess, and otherwise wasting time. Unfortunately, bad things *do* happen on college campuses, and not always to somebody else.

In the fall of 2012, an 18 year old freshman named Philip enrolled at a university a couple of hours away from his hometown. Philip's parents were both college graduates and his two older brothers had also attended college. At 6 feet 5 inches, Philip was a large guy (often referred to by his many friends as a big loveable teddy bear), someone who by all appearances "would be able hold his liquor." Philip had attended a private high school, had played defensive tackle on his high school's football team, was chosen homecoming king, and was very active in his local church. He was a fun-loving guy with a steady girlfriend he hoped to one day marry. And by all accounts from his high school friends, Philip was not a partyer. Nevertheless, he found himself at a rush event for a campus fraternity the second week of college, and the result was tragic. After attending a dinner for new pledges, an eager group of 15 young men, including Philip, were locked in a room in a fraternity house and told that they could not leave until several bottles of hard liquor in the room had been consumed. What happened next eventually came out during police investigations and court hearings. During a short period of time, Philip ingested the equivalent of 36 shots of hard liquor. Seeing his deteriorating condition, some of the others present asked him, "Are you OK?" to which he responded, "No." Philip then passed out. Thinking that he just needed to sleep it off, several fraternity brothers dragged him to "The Sober Up Room" (also called "The Drunk Room") where he was supposed to be watched by some fraternity members, but left him there alone. Approximately three hours later, the fraternity brothers found him not breathing, started CPR and called for an ambulance. Philip died of alcohol poisoning his second week of college.

I found out about Philip because he was the son of a dear friend of mine. He put a face to the problem of binge drinking and the danger of alcohol poisoning on college campuses across the country for me. Having two sons of my own, I could sense the heartbreak of my friend. This was one lesson I wished I did not have to learn. As a result of Philip's death, the university he attended instituted an expanded Alcohol Awareness Program. Two of the fraternity brothers involved were sentenced to jail time, and the parents of others involved were forced to pay hundreds of thousands of dollars in fines and court costs. Unbelievably, another student at the same university had died six years before from the same thing – alcohol poisoning. A subsequent lawsuit noted, "If fraternity members had called 9-1-1 when Dhanens collapsed instead of hours later, his life could have been saved." (http://www.fresnobee)

Many colleges require their new students to attend an information session on Alcohol Awareness during New Student Orientation sessions. It's easy in the rush of pre-semester activities to ignore the information being presented. <u>Nevertheless, make a commitment to learning about the dangers of binge drinking and the signs of alcohol poisoning. The information might help you to save the life of a friend, or even your own.</u>

According to author Dave Ellis, "In the United States, alcohol is still the number one drug of choice and becoming intoxicated is still the primary motive for alcohol use." (Ellis, Chapter 11). Here are some alarming statistics:

- Four out of five college students drink alcohol, and half of these admit to abusing alcohol

- "31% (of college students) met (the) criteria for a diagnosis of alcohol abuse"

- One fourth of college students report they have experienced negative "consequences to their drinking... including doing poorly on exams... and receiving lower grades overall"

- A half a million students are "unintentionally injured under the influence of alcohol"

- "at least 1400 college deaths a year are related to alcohol"
  (www.collegedrinkingprevention.gov)

In the article "The Dark Power of Fraternities," Caitlin Flanagan writes, "Across the country, kids fall-disastrously- from the upper heights of fraternity houses with some regularity."

In 1985 a student "grievously injured in a Kappa Alpha-related accident reached a settlement with the fraternity that, over the course of his lifetime, could amount to $21 million..."

In 2009 a tri-Delta pledge fell from a "third floor 'sleeping porch' to the cement approximately 25 feet below" resulting in severe brain damage that forced her to have to learn to walk and dress herself again (and ending her college career and her aspirations to become a Veterinarian).

In February 2012 a student at U.C. Berkeley "attempted to climb down the drainpipe of the Phi Gamma Delta house, fell, and suffered devastating injuries."

In April 2012, "a 21-year-old student at Gannon University in Pennsylvania died after a fall from a second floor balcony of the Alpha Phi Delta house the night before..."

In Fall 2013 an M.I.T. student was seriously injured "after falling through a skylight at the Phi Sigma Kappa house and landing some 40 feet below."

In August 2013 Wesleyan University and Beta Theta Pi settled a $10 million lawsuit by Jane Doe, a freshman raped at a 2010 Halloween party. (Alcohol is frequently involved in cases of sexual assault on college campuses.)

Ms. Flanagan states, "...since 2005 more than 60 people- the majority of them students- have died in incidents linked to fraternities..."

CAUTION

What are some things you can do to educate yourself about alcohol? How can you be sure that when you walk across the stage at graduation to receive your diploma, you aren't also walking away with a drug or alcohol addiction you did not have when you started college?

Here are some suggestions:

- Participate in Alcohol Awareness Programs during New Student Orientation. Pay attention to the videos, online resources and speakers.

- Think proactively about situations that could trip you up, and plan for how you will respond to them.

- Know your limits.

- Agree to be the designated driver, and abstain from drinking alcohol to make sure you and your friends arrive home safely.

- Practice saying "no" ahead of time so you won't be forced into unwanted situations.

- Strategically avoid events and activities where you feel you'll be pressured into doing something you'll later regret.

- Plan alternate social activities with like-minded individuals- take a night out to see a funny movie, purchase tickets to see a campus play or concert, become involved with campus ministries related to your religious background, take a weekend hike, or organize a barbecue or potluck.

Know The Signs Of Alcohol Poisoning

A person who is or may be in danger of alcohol poisoning may exhibit the following: "Confusion, vomiting, seizures, slow breathing (less than eight breaths a minute), irregular breathing (a gap of more than 10 seconds between breaths), blue-tinged or pale skin, low body temperature (hypothermia), and/ or passing out (unconsciousness) and can't be awakened. A person who is unconscious or can't be awakened is at risk of dying." (http://mayoclinic.org/diseases-conditions/alcohol-poisoning/basics/symptoms)

A person who has alcohol poisoning that goes untreated: Can choke "on his or her own vomit," has irregular breathing or stops breathing, has an irregular or no heartbeat, experiences hypothermia, or hypoglycemia that leads to seizures, and can experience "seizures, permanent brain damage or death." "Rapid binge drinking (which often happens on a bet or dare) is especially dangerous because the victim can ingest a fatal dose before becoming unconscious." (http://www.collegedrinkingprevention.gov/OtherAlcoholInformation/factsAboutAlcohol)

The following mnemonic can help you to remember the signs of alcohol poisoning:

M	Mental Confusion
U	Unresponsive
S	Snoring/Gasping for Air
T	Throwing up
H	Hypothermia
E	Erratic Breathing
L	Loss of Consciousness
P	Paleness/Blueness of Skin

(http://awareawakealive.org/knowthesigns)

"Binge drinking, which can lead to alcohol poisoning, occurs when a woman drinks four or more alcoholic beverages at one occasion. For a man, consuming five or more drinks is considered to be binge drinking." (http://www.projectknow.com/research/alcohol poisoning/)

If you suspect someone may be at risk for alcohol poisoning:

- ☐ Get help! Call 911 (if possible, relay the type of alcohol the person has consumed and the quantity).

- ☐ Never leave someone who is unconscious alone.

- ☐ If the person is vomiting, try to have him or her sit up. "If the person must lie down, make sure to turn his or her head to the side- this helps prevent choking."

- ☐ "Try to keep the person awake to prevent the loss of consciousness."

- ☐ It is better to risk offending a friend by calling for help if you suspect they are at risk of alcohol poisoning, than to ignore the problem and end up with a friend who becomes seriously injured or even dies as a result.

(http://mayoclinic.org/diseases-conditions/alcohol-poisoning/basics/symptoms)

TIP: Make a commitment to learning about the dangers of binge drinking and the signs of alcohol poisoning!!! The information might help you to save the life of a friend, or even your own.

Case Study: Wasted Days & Wasted Nights

Life was moving faster in college than Aaron ever thought it would. He knew college would be different than high school, but he never imagined he could have so much fun while being a student. Early in his freshman year he rushed the biggest fraternity on campus, known for their weekend parties that began on Thursday nights, and for the throngs of women that frequented their social events. Aaron had come from a somewhat conservative middle class family. Both his parents had attended college, and held rewarding jobs; his father was an engineer and his mother worked as a real estate agent. They were thrilled when Aaron was accepted to their alma mater, and knew that with his academic background, outgoing personality, and their professional contacts, that he was on his way to having the same middle class life style that they enjoyed. The summer before his freshman year, Aaron's dad had given him just one caveat- "Four years, Aaron. You have four years to finish your Bachelor's degree. Your mom and I have saved enough money to pay for your tuition and living expenses without you having to work or take out any loans." Aaron knew his younger brother would start college in two years, and his sister would follow a year later. His parents had been diligent about starting college savings accounts for them when they were little, and they were confident that their three children would earn college degrees and build on the financial success they had established.

Aaron's university operated on the quarter system and he knew he would have to get down to business right away in order to keep up with the fast pace. HIs mother had even gone as far as to draw up a chart outlining the classes he would need to take to graduate in four years, and the order in which he should enroll in them. Unlike many of his classmates, he entered college knowing exactly what to take. He had even looked over the college catalog and selected the General Education classes he wanted to take which would strengthen his chosen career-Financial Planning. He'd selected the Business major at his university because it was ranked one of the top programs in the country. He also planned on spending one quarter in an internship with a top firm on the East Coast to seal his future in the field. His parents had friends who could help him make the professional contacts he would need to enter the competitive field of Finance. He knew if he landed a job with a particular company, they would pay for his M.B.A. program. He had it all planned out- a few years working in the field, an impressive graduate degree, and he would sail to the top of his field, stock options in hand.

Mid-term exams and finals came fast that first quarter. Aaron was so busy spending his evenings frequenting college parties in pursuit of women, that studying took a back seat to everything else. He did force himself to get to the library right before finals, and marveled at his ability to cram all his studying into just a few weeks. Whereas in high school he always had to head home after going out with his friends, in college he could stay out all night and his parents were none the wiser. He brushed off his 2.0 GPA at the end of his freshman year as inconsequential because he was "still getting adjusted to college life." He told himself he'd do better the next year, knowing he needed to bring his GPA way up in order to compete for the internship he wanted to complete during his junior year. He managed to keep his grades secret from his parents, and assured them that he was doing fine and that he loved college. When his mother tried to follow him on social media, he told her he didn't spend much time on the Internet because he was too busy studying. He panicked when he realized that she might see pictures of him and his frat brothers in his various online photo albums with titles such as "Where's the party?!" When he went home for the summer after his freshman year, he realized that he had built up such a tolerance for drinking that he could go out with his old high school friends, down several beers and some mixed drinks, and still keep his parents from knowing exactly how much he liked to party.

By the start of his sophomore year, Aaron had been selected as one of three vice presidents of his fraternity; he was assigned the task of recruiting new members and coordinating the next Rush activities. His frat buddies were amazed out how he could party harder than everyone else. If the frat down the street was serving a certain amount of alcohol, he made sure his frat offered twice as much at their events. If the other frats planned to have a DJ for their party, he'd find a band who could play for his frat's party. He came up with themed parties that became the talk of the campus. His lists of Friends on social media swelled. On most days he walked around campus thinking, "This is the life!" so he was shocked when in the middle of his sophomore year, he received a letter from the University Advising Center that stated "You have been placed on Academic Probation due to your GPA falling below a 2.0. If your GPA does not increase to a minimum of 2.0 by the end of your sophomore year, you will be dismissed from the University for a period of one year. During that time, you may enroll at a community college to raise your GPA, and submit a petition to reenroll at the University. Please contact the Advising Center immediately to discuss your academic progress with one of our advisors."

When he confided to Nick, one of his frat housemates that he was starting to feel like he might have taken on too much, Nick took him to his room and pulled open his dresser drawer. It was loaded with prescription pills. "Whoa! Where'd you get all THAT?!" Aaron shouted. "My dad's a doctor," responded Nick. "Whatever I want, I can get. In fact I've been supplying half the guys on Greek Row for the last few years. I can set you up with whatever you need for a small fee." While Aaron loved having a reputation of being able to hold his liquor, he'd prided himself on the fact that he didn't do drugs. He had a bright career ahead of him and he didn't want to jeopardize his future by getting addicted to any hard stuff or by getting in trouble with the law. He knew his parents would flip if they found out the about the extent of his partying, and he didn't want to make things worse. "Come on, Aaron. These won't hurt you. They'll just give you the energy you need to stay up late studying before exams. Everybody's using something! How do you think I've managed to get through college all these years?" Aaron hesitated when Nick offered him a few pills. He imagined the look on his parents face if they found out he was on Academic Probation. They'd been hounding him about filling out the internship applications and had even made phone calls on his behalf to make sure his name would be recognized when he applied for those coveted internships. He pictured their angst if they could see how he'd really been spending his time in college. "Here, try these. You'll see they'll help you to concentrate and you won't have to give up any parties because you have to hit the books." Aaron tried to turn down Nick's offer but stopped cold when Nick said, "You know, your name has come up over and over again as the next President of the fraternity. Elections are coming up in a few months. I'm backing you 'cause I think you've got what it takes to hold the top job. Life's only going to get harder the older you get. I know you have your eye on that internship and you're going to have to have good grades if you want to get into

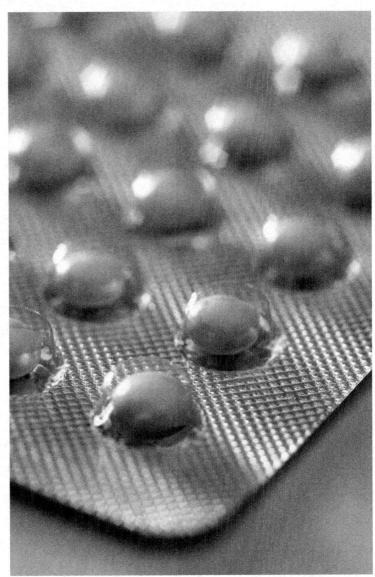

grad school. You're going to have to pull a lot of all-nighters to get the rewards you want in life. These will help you to get it all done." "Here," Nick said as he pressed some pills into Aaron's hand. "Consider these a gift. I've got more, if you need 'em." As Nick walked away, Aaron's cellphone buzzed. His mom had just texted him. "Guess what?! We'll be passing by campus this weekend. So excited Dad & I finally get to see where u live & meet your friends. Let's plan on dinner on Sat. Can u show your sister around campus Sun.? She's going too & wants to check out the campus before she starts writing her personal statement for her college applications (she likes the idea of following in your footsteps). Answer me. Mom."

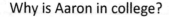

Why is Aaron in college?

If things continue as they are for Aaron:

What is the best case scenario for him?

What is the worst case scenario?

What is the most likely scenario for Aaron?

What has worked in favor of Aaron being successful in college?

What has worked against Aaron being successful in college?

What advice would you give Aaron to improve his situation?

Self-Assessment

Rate yourself on the behaviors of successful students on a scale of 1 – 5. How well prepared are you in the following areas?

     1 = I need lots of help with this

     2 = I could do better in this area

     3 = I'm OK in this area

     4 = I do a good job in this area

     5 = I'm very good at this

STAYING HEALTHY IN COLLEGE

____ I have talked to my family members about what is expected of me in college so that they can support me

____ I have access to medical care through insurance or the campus Health Center

____ I pay attention to how I feel physically to prevent getting overly-stressed

____ I am not afraid to ask for help when I need it (e.g., tutoring)

____ I have a network of friends or know of campus professionals I can turn to when I need emotional support

____ I have a healthy self esteem (I feel good about myself and understand the triggers that can lower my self esteem)

____ I am familiar with tips for personal safety

____ I know what to do in the event of a campus emergency

____ I know how to recognize the signs of Alcohol Poisoning and I know what to do if someone is exhibiting these signs

____ I avoid binge drinking, and I am willing to abstain from drinking and be the designated driver when going out with my friends.

Place a checkmark next to any items that you rated a 1 (I need lots of help with this) or a 2 (I could do better in this area). Identify where you could go on campus in order to solicit help and learn more about staying healthy in college.

The following information can help you to stay safe and healthy, and to build a support network in college.

- Become familiar with your professors' office hours, free or low cost tutoring services available on campus, and the resources available to you at your campus Health Center early in your academic career.

- List the names and phone numbers of some friends, peer advisors, or counseling professionals that you can talk to should you begin to feel stressed or overloaded.

- If you haven't done so, send a short note to your friends or family members outlining the activities you will be involved in this term and letting them know that you may not be able to accept every invitation that comes your way. Thank them in advance for supporting your educational goals.

- Take some time to become familiar with campus safety procedures. Know what to do in case of a fire drill, a campus lockdown, or other type of emergency. Program the phone numbers to the Campus Police, Fire Department and Emergency Service into your phone. Know the location of emergency call boxes on campus that connect you to emergency personnel, and take advantage of late night campus escort services when walking to and from your dorm or your car.

- Travel with one or two others or a small group when attending social events and parties; make sure that everyone in the group agrees not to leave anyone behind.

- Have a small network of friends who are familiar with your routine who would notice if something seems unusual. Do a nightly check in via text or email to a trusted family member or friend so that they know you are OK.

> *This chapter is dedicated to my friend Diane,*
> *her husband and two sons,*
> *who miss Philip every day.*

Chapter Notes:

Things to think about...

Things to remember...

Things to do....

Chapter 12

Play For Life
(Developing Transferable Skills)

"Nothing is impossible, the word itself says 'I'm possible!'"

Audrey Hepburn

Transferring From A Community College To A University

The following section (pages 236 - 245) is for students who are enrolled in a community college and are thinking about transferring to a four year college or university to complete a Bachelor's or four year degree. Transferring can be a confusing process. You will want to work closely with Academic Counselors and Transfer Advisors to make sure that the courses you are taking will enable you to transfer to another college in a timely manner (i.e., without taking extra or unnecessary courses). Your campus may have a Transfer Center or Transfer Counselors that work specifically with students wishing to transfer. Make sure you take advantage of all available resources so that the transfer process is smooth and clear cut.

Myth #11 - If you start earning your four year degree at a community college, you'll be at a disadvantage compared to students who attended the university all four years.

Research indicates that students who start at a community college and the transfer to a university to complete their Bachelor's degree actually do better academically than students who started at the university as freshmen. Specifically, they tend to drop out less and finish their degrees faster. Some students are concerned that they might not receive as good of an education at a community college as a at university. However, it is important to note that there are great professors (and some not so good professors) on every college campus. At a large university you might attend numerous classes in large lecture halls with as many as 600 students. Sometimes your courses at a university may be taught by graduate students instead of professors. In a community college, your class sizes tend to be smaller and you have a good chance of interacting with your professors, if you want to do so. Community college professors do not have as much pressure to publish as university professors, so they are able to dedicate more of their time to actual classroom teaching. Many instructors specifically chose to work at a community college because they want to concentrate their efforts on classroom teaching, as opposed to conducting research.

KEY CONCEPT: You get out of college what you put into it.

TOP 10 REASONS TO TRANSFER TO A UNIVERSITY

1. The more education you have, the more money you'll make.

2. The more education you have, the more career opportunities you'll have.

3. You can select a campus that fits your personality.

4. There's Financial Aid to help pay your way.

5. There are thousands of four year colleges and universities to select from (if you consider applying to out of state institutions and campuses in other countries).

6. You'll be exposed to graduate education opportunities (M.A., M.D., M.B.A., Ph.D., J.D., etc.).

7. You'll get to meet people from all over the world.

8. You can participate in intercollegiate activities and intramural sports teams, or join one or more of hundreds of student clubs and organizations.

9. You can earn a Bachelor's Degree in Computer Science, Dairy Science, or Social Science (just to name a few...).

10. You get to live in a dorm!!!

50 Tips For Transferring To A University

Here are some helpful tips if you plan to start your education at a community college and then transfer to a university to complete your degree.

- Start researching transfer options while you are still in high school.

- Review the cost-effectiveness of the transfer route. How much money will you save off the total cost of your Bachelor's degree if you transfer from a community college? Attending a local community college and then transferring to a local university while living at home is often the least expensive path to complete a four year degree; this is an excellent option for students looking to minimize student loan debt. You can cut the cost of completing a Bachelor's degree almost in half by taking this route.

- Remember that you rule out your chance of being accepted to a college if you don't apply! Consider applying to out-of-state campuses, too. The more campuses you apply to, the greater your chance of being accepted. Apply to more than one university, unless you have signed a Guaranteed Transfer Admission Agreement with a specific campus and have met all the requirements to be guaranteed admission.

- Do not believe myths such as "If you earn a two year degree, you can automatically transfer to a university."

- Remember that students that transfer perform as well or better at the university than native freshmen!

- Remember that you start with a clean slate at a community college. Don't assume because you messed up in high school that you can't start over. If you transfer to a university, they generally won't consider your high school grades in the admissions decision.

- Look online for up-to-date lists of courses articulated between your community college and four year colleges (e.g., in California, the primary source for online articulation agreement is the ASSIST database). Ask your academic advisor for other ways to access formal articulation agreements between colleges, including agreements between your community college and private universities.

- Use the on-line course planning features on on-line applications; start an application, save it, and go back to it later to continue working on it.

- Visit your college Transfer Center—there are great resources there to help you learn more about your transfer options Attend workshops on transfer options or sign up to participate in campus-sponsored fieldtrips to four year universities. Look for fliers on transfer events on campus bulletin boards.

- Research Guaranteed Transfer Programs with local universities (these may be referred to as Transfer Admissions Agreements or Transfer Admissions Guarantee).

- Research how each course listed on your community college Educational Plan transfers, as well as which area of General Education it meets (Written Communication, Math & Science, Humanities, etc.). Also check to see if courses you are taking fulfill pre-major requirements or university graduation requirements.

- Interview someone who transferred to a university in your major/discipline.

- Look up the transfer links on your community college's website.

- Work with your Academic Advisor to select your classes, and make sure you have an up-to-date Educational Plan.

- Don't try to guess the transfer requirements of different universities; be sure to obtain accurate information by checking with Transfer Counselors & college catalogs.

- Remember that you generally will submit transfer admissions applications almost a year prior to enrolling in the university.

- Complete the FAFSA as the first step in applying for Financial Aid (submit the FAFSA in January for following academic year). Be sure to request that copies of your information be forwarded to each university to which you apply (they will need this information in order to determine your Financial Aid package should you be accepted).

- Find out which of your instructors transferred from a community college to a university and ask them to share their experience and advice.

- Review the syllabus for each course you take to better understand how your classes meet transfer requirements.

- Research how your courses fulfill the major prep requirements for different majors/ schools. Note: The same major can have very different lower division or pre-major requirements at different campuses. Don't assume that a transfer plan for one campus will be the same as that of another campus, even if the colleges are part of the same organizational system.

- Consider transferring to a private college, as many can offer you an excellent Financial Aid package. You may be surprised to learn that attending a private university may cost even less than attending a public institution, due to the additional Financial Aid you are offered.

- Never assume that you can't afford to transfer to a private school, or research university. The higher the overall cost of a degree, the more likely you will be eligible for Financial Aid.

- Visit your professors during their office hours to learn more about how your classes tie in with Bachelor's Degree requirements.

- Invite a university instructor or former transfer students to speak to your class or student club about strategies for successful transfer.

- Find out the dates of annual events on your community college campus such as "Transfer Day" (a college fair where university representatives talk to students about transfer options and procedures).

- Research the names, phone numbers, and email addresses of the Transfer Advisors at local universities.

- Review the articulation agreements in your major —which ones exist?

- Ask faculty to work towards articulating additional courses in your major with local universities.

- Identify obstacles/barriers that could get in your way of transferring to a university, and actively work to prevent or eliminate these.

- Keep an on-going list of questions you have about transfer; email these to your Transfer Advisor, or make an appointment with him or her to ask all your questions at once.

- Review current copies of the catalogs from each campus where you intend to apply as a transfer student. Your community college Transfer Center may have hard copies on file, or you can access these online.

- Find out what you can do with an advanced degree in your field. What additional job opportunities would you have if you earned a Master's Degree or Doctorate? Research the salary ranges in your future field/career for people with varying levels of education.

- If you are struggling academically, be sure to take advantage of campus tutoring services. A higher grade point average will help you to be more competitive in the transfer process.

- Begin to think early in your college career about pursuing a graduate degree (i.e., education beyond the four-year degree). If you transfer from a community college to a university, you may be completing graduate school applications by the Fall Semester of your senior year.

- Talk to university advisors if you are planning on eventually completing a teaching credential; teacher credential programs have very specific requirements in order for students to meet state requirements (and these can vary from state to state). Look up the credential requirements for local school districts if you are considering becoming a teacher.

- If you are interested in becoming a teacher, research fast-track options for students sponsored by local school districts and universities.

- If you are working full-time and wish to complete a Bachelor's degree, become familiar with local transfer programs for working adults (i.e., private schools that offer evening, weekend, and online classes for working students).

- Attend campus programs that recognize successful transfer students (receptions, awards ceremonies) to help keep you motivated!

- Find out if your campus has a Transfer Achievement Certificate or two year degree in University Transfer.

- Once you have been accepted to a university, remember not to let your grades slip! Your admissions offers could be revoked if you earn poor grades your last year or semester at the community college.

- Identify 10 universities that accept transfers in your discipline. What are their transfer requirements?

- Visit different universities during vacations and summer breaks. Take tours of the campuses, and talk to current students to find out what they like about their campuses.

- Whenever possible, research questions related to transfer yourself to help prepare for the university (this will help you to become independent and assertive- traits that will be helpful in the university environment).

- Meet with university departmental advisors while still enrolled in community college.

- Schedule an appointment with visiting university recruiters. Many community colleges post schedules of university recruiters who are visiting your campus.

- Become aware of transfer statistics that might affect you (e.g., the typical entering grade point average of transfers in your major).

- Find out if other local community colleges have lower division courses that transfer to your intended university; enroll in these courses if your own campus is limited in the transfer courses they offer.

- Commit to three things you will do each semester to learn more about the transfer process.

- Research which careers are currently in demand, such Teaching, Engineering, and Nursing, and find out which universities offer four year degrees in these areas.

- Elaborate on extenuating circumstances, challenges, or obstacles you have had to overcome when submitting admissions or scholarship applications. You may be able to include this information in your personal statement.

Transfer Assignment

Use the following questions as a guide when attending your community college's "Transfer Day" (University Admissions Fair). Interview representatives from at least three different universities. Include at least one state college and one private university. (If your college does not sponsor a Transfer Day event, consult university catalogs or websites to obtain this information.)

1) Name of campus / location

2) Deadline to apply for next Fall Semester

3) What is the application process (e.g., required test scores, personal statement, letters of recommendation from instructors, etc.)?

4) Cost of attending (include tuition, room & board, books, transportation)

5) Does this college/university offer your major?

6) Unique features (e.g., teacher/student ratio, national rankings, Study Abroad programs)

Checklist: Things You Should Find Out If You Plan To Transfer To A University

- If transfer advisors from the university you want to attend regularly visit your community college to recruit students

- Which courses are transferable

- Whether you can complete all of your General Education requirements at the community college level and transfer to the university "G.E. Certified"

- Which universities will accept the pattern of General Education courses you are following

- The maximum number of lower division units the university will accept towards your four year degree

- The number of upper division units you will be required to complete

- Whether you have completed the requirements for a 2 year degree in the process of taking transfer courses

- Whether the university you plan to attend has housing designated for transfer students

KEY CONCEPT: University transfer doesn't just happen- you must plan carefully to reach your goal.

Myth #12 - The degree you earn will determine the jobs you can get after you graduate.

When it comes to selecting a major, you will have many choices. Some students think that if they earn a degree in a particular area- Business, for example- that they will have to work in the Business field the rest of their life. In reality, many students enter careers that don't have any clear connection to their college major. Employers are looking for a wide array of skills or competencies in new employees, such as strong communication skills and the ability to learn new material quickly, to take direction, to work in groups, to lead others and to bring a fresh perspective to their workforce. Many students complete a 2 or 4 year degree, work a few years, and then go back to school for another degree, such as a Master's Degree or Ph.D. If you ask employers, they'll most likely say that having a college degree is almost always better than not having one. Many employers will require a Bachelor's Degree, at a minimum, for applicants seeking employment with them. They may use this as a screening mechanism because they believe that someone with a few years of college under their belt will make a better employee than someone with only a high school diploma (i.e., they'll be able to write better, solve problems, and have stronger technical skills).

"The average American worker changes careers 3 – 5 times in a lifetime.'" (Capital Public Radio)

College Is The Time To Develop Transferable Skills

Do you want to approach future job interviews knowing that you have the right skills to get hired or promoted? Besides the knowledge you will learn in college that may be specific to your career area, such as accounting, engineering, nursing, or teaching skills (often called "hard skills"), what kinds of things do employers look for in new hires? How can you make sure you stand out over all the other applicants competing for jobs? Many years ago the U.S. Government issued a report entitled "The Secretary's Commission on Achieving Necessary Skills" or "SCANS" for short. Essentially, this report outlined the skills that employers wanted their new hires (recent college graduates) to have. These included skills such as working well with others, having good communication skills, making good use of resources such as time and money, thinking creatively, knowing how to solve problems, and understanding how to use technology to complete tasks.

Years later, these skills, often referred to as "soft skills" are still in high demand by employers. Luckily, these skills are transferable- you can take them with you from job to job. Indeed, your soft skills should grow over time, just like your job-specific skills or knowledge. While you may be new to working in teams in your first job, by the time you've worked 10 or 20 years and have held a variety of jobs, your skills at being a good team member and knowing how to work effectively in a team setting and lead a team of employees should have increased, as well.

College is a great time to develop your soft skills. Each time you take the lead in a study group, or run for a student government office, or take on a leadership position in a student club, you have the opportunity to strengthen your soft skills. Think of someone you know who is a good leader. What kinds of skills do they have? How do they interact with others, run meetings, approach problem solving, and work through different tasks? Chances are they weren't just born a good leader, although they may have some natural talent at motivating and guiding others. They most likely have developed their leadership skills by holding a variety of leadership positions and by practicing their goal setting, decision making, and time management skills.

Use the following pages to assess how well you are doing in the skills outlined in the SCANS Report. Then, identify how you can strengthen any areas where your scores are not as high as you would like them to be.

What Employers Want In College Graduates

Rate yourself on the following areas on a scale of 1 – 10 (1 = completely disagree, 10 = strongly agree).

Identifying, organizing, planning and allocating resources:

_____ I spend my time working on activities that will help me to accomplish my goals. I know how to manage my time, and make and follow schedules.

_____ I know how to prepare budgets, predict future costs, keep good records, and adjust budgets to achieve goals.

_____ I know how to make good use of resources such as space and materials.

_____ When working with others, I know how to assess their strengths and give them work based on their strengths.

_____ I know how to evaluate the work performance of others and give them feedback on their work.

Working with others:

_____ When working with a team, I actively contribute to meeting the group's goals.

_____ I am good at teaching others new skills.

_____ I am good at working with customers and meeting their needs.

_____ I am good at communicating my ideas to others, and convincing others that my ideas are good.

_____ When I see something that needs to be improved, I know how to propose changes without threatening others.

_____ I am good at getting others to reach agreement when they have different or competing interests.

_____ I am good at working with people from a variety of backgrounds and cultures.

Acquiring and using information:

_____ I am good at acquiring and evaluating information.

_____ I am good at organizing information and keeping records.

_____ I am good at interpreting information and communicating it to others.

_____ I know how to use computers to process information.

Understanding complex interrelationships:

_____ I understand how social, organizational and technological systems function, and I can work effectively with them.

_____ I am good at figuring out trends, predicting how they will impact operations, and figuring out problems so they can be corrected.

_____ I am good at suggesting how to improve systems (e.g., methods, procedures) and developing new systems to improve work performance.

Working with a variety of technologies:

_____ I am good at selecting the right procedures, tools or equipment to complete a task, including computers and computer software.

_____ I am good at understanding the purpose of equipment, as well as how to set-up and operate equipment.

_____ I am good at preventing problems, identifying problems, or solving problems with equipment such as computers.

- **Where did you score the highest? List a couple of examples to illustrate that you are strong in those areas.**

- **Where did you score the lowest? List some strategies you could use to improve your performance in those areas.**

The Secretary's Commission on Achieving Necessary Skills (SCANS): U.S. Department of Labor

Rate yourself on the following areas on a scale of 1 – 10 (1 = completely disagree, 10 = strongly agree).

Basic Skills:

_____ I am good at understanding written information, including instructional manuals, graphs, and schedules.

_____ I am good at communicating my thoughts and ideas, and information and messages in writing.

_____ I am good at creating documents such as letters, written directions, manuals, reports, graphs and flow charts.

_____ I am good at performing basic math computations. I know how to select the right mathematical technique to solve a problem.

_____ I am good at listening to, interpreting, and responding to verbal messages and other cues.

_____ I am good at organizing my ideas and communicating them verbally.

Thinking Skills:

_____ I am good at creative thinking. I am good at coming up with new ideas.

_____ I know how to identify clear goals, brainstorm possible solutions, and evaluate and select the best alternative.

_____ I am good at recognizing problems, and coming up with plans to solve them.

_____ I am good at organizing and processing information including symbols, pictures, graphs, etc.

_____ I know how to learn new material. I know how to use different learning techniques to acquire and apply new knowledge and skills.

_____ I have good reasoning skills. I can see how rules and principles exist and apply them to solving problems.

Personal Qualities:

_____ I am responsible. I work hard to achieve goals.

_____ I believe that I am a worthy person. I have a strong self-esteem.

_____ I am sociable. I am understanding, friendly, adaptable, empathetic, and polite in group settings.

_____ I am good at managing myself. I am good at assessing myself, setting personal goals, monitoring progress towards my goals, and exhibiting self control.

_____ I am honest. I choose ethical courses of action.

- **Where did you score the highest? List a couple of examples to illustrate that you are strong in those areas.**

- **Where did you score the lowest? List some strategies you could use to improve your performance in those areas.**

KEY CONCEPT: The students sitting next to you in class today may become valuable professional contacts for you when you graduate.

Developing Your Professional Network

The same networking that will help you to get through college will prove invaluable when you start job hunting. Networking (the human kind) is one of those transferable skills that you can develop while at a college or university. While you won't necessarily ever enroll in a class entitled "Effective Professional Networking," you can definitely practice and perfect the art of networking during your student years.

Remember that you are building your professional network from Day #1 of college. Every roommate, dorm acquaintance, professor, classmate, study group partner, or friend from a student organization is a potential contact in the professional network you will need to tap once you graduate from college and enter the permanent workforce. Make sure your professional profile appears on websites such as LinkedIn. Also think twice about the type of pictures and information you post on social media websites, as you never know when a prospective employer will decide to look you up on Facebook or some other site to see what you're really like (and whether they should offer you a job). Regularly spend time sustaining your professional network. Send holiday or birthday greetings to your contacts, post updates on your educational and/or professional achievements, and congratulate others on their accomplishments.

I owe at least two of the jobs I obtained to my broad professional network. One of the best pieces of advice I received when I was in college was, "Tell *everyone* you know when you are looking for a job." Twice in my career when I needed a job, I decided to test the idea I'd learned in college. The first time, I sent out emails to many of my professional contacts informing them I was job hunting, not really knowing if it would work or not. Then a month later, I received a phone call from the Dean at a college about 30 miles from where I lived. He introduced himself and said, "I heard you were looking for work, and I need someone to run our Career and Transfer Center. Would you be interested?" It turned out that he had put the word out that he needed a new staff person, and two of the people I'd contacted told him "Call Sharon- she's looking for work!" I ended up working at that campus for 3 ½ years. The second time I needed a job I sent out emails and made phone calls to friends and professional acquaintances. One day, my friend Maria who taught at a local university called me from her cell phone as she hurriedly walked across campus. She said, "Sharon, I just heard, there's a job opening in the College of Business. Check it out!" I quickly went online to look up the job and applied for it. I certainly would have missed the job announcement if she had not called me. I was offered a very interesting job overseeing an advising center for 4500 undergraduate Business majors, which I would say was one of the highlights of my career. Now when students tell me they're looking for a job, I share the advice I received- "Tell everyone you know that you are job hunting." Try this the next time you need a new job- it's sure to work!

Charting Your Career: Career Ladder

Students can often articulate where they will be in 20 years. They know the type of job they want, where they want to live, and perhaps even which type of car they will drive. However, if you ask them to articulate *how* they are going to get from here to there, they often can't fill in the details.

Drafting a career ladder can help you to visualize the steps you need to take to reach your long-term goals. Each rung on the "ladder" represents a different step that you will need to take to eventually achieve your academic and/or career goals.

Exercise:

Take a long piece of butcher paper (about 6 feet) and lay it flat on a table. Get some different colored marking pens.

At the top of the paper, state where you would like to be in 20 years; specifically, what type of job do you envision yourself having?

Starting at the bottom of the paper, begin to list the steps you need to take to begin to reach your long-term career goal. What is important here is that you fill in as much detail as possible. Writing "Earn my degree" on the bottom rung is too general. A better approach would be to draw 20 or more rungs and then slowly fill in the information. Each rung could represent a year, or a major step in moving closer towards your long term goals.

A key feature of this exercise is to help you to understand that you don't just fall into your dream job. You usually have to hold a series of jobs with increasing experience; this starts in college! If you want to become a doctor, you should probably steer clear of college jobs or summer employment working in the university cafeteria or library. A better series of jobs for you (while in college) might look like this:

* Work at Information Desk at campus Health Center

* Hold a summer internship at local clinic educating parents on the importance of vaccinating their children

* Attend a summer school program sponsored by a medical school

* Obtain a job working in an emergency room

* Volunteer at a summer camp for children with disabilities

The time to start building valuable work experience is while you are in college. You should not wait until after you graduate to try out jobs in your field. Early exposure to the world of work may help you to decide if you really want to pursue a particular field. The chances of a pre-med student getting into medical school are stronger if s/he can demonstrate that they have some work experience related to the health field.

The lower rungs of the ladder should include information such as the major courses of study you want to complete, college jobs and summer employment. Next you would list any graduate school programs you plan to complete. The mid-section of rungs represent the jobs you will have when you first enter your career field. Use this exercise to identify a series of positions or training experiences that will help you to get to where you ultimately want to arrive in 20 years. Post the butcher paper on your bedroom wall to serve as a visual reminder of your long term goals.

Myth #13 - Once you graduate from college, you'll be able to land your dream job.

The unofficial motto of my alma mater was "Study. Work hard. Get rich." Unfortunately, it isn't always true that a Bachelor's degree will lead to a great job or career, at least not immediately after graduation. Most employees have to pay their dues by starting with entry level jobs, and then have to work their way up to higher paying or more appealing positions. My first job was running a dorm at a major university. While that was a great learning experience, the work I do now is more rewarding than that first job I took, and it also pays much better. Sometime students are shocked to graduate and then experience great difficulty landing a job in their field. For some graduates it's easy for them to give up on their chosen career early in the game. Recent college graduates should expect to spend weeks and even months applying for jobs to acquire something that is to their liking. They may have to take an entry level job somewhere and perform well in that position for a year or two before they can begin to apply for jobs that are more to their liking, more in line with their career choice, or have higher pay. That can be very frustrating when you have a degree in Engineering, Architecture or Nursing. While the chances of finding a job in your field that pays well increases with earning a college degree, the degree is not a guarantee that you will see rewards immediately after graduation. Having work experience related to your field or having held an internship can give your job hunt a big boost.

10 Year Resume Exercise

The following exercise can help you to envision where you would like to be educationally and professionally 10 years from now. Use the blank form as a sample and fill in the relevant information. Print a copy of this resume and post it on your bedroom wall or somewhere you will see it frequently. This will serve as a visual reminder of what you want to accomplish.

Fill in the form as follows:

Top right hand corner	Write today's date 10 years from now (e.g., Sept. 1, 2025.)
Underneath that	Write your age 10 years from today.
Name	Will your name be the same 10 years from now?
Address	Where will you be living in 10 years?
Email address	What will it be in 10 years?
Educational background	What type of degrees, certificates, and/or licenses will you have earned? Which schools will you have attended? List the dates for all degrees earned.
Employment History	List most recent job first. Include job title, the name of the company and dates of employment.
Professional Competencies	List special skills you have, as well as major accomplishments.
Professional Affiliations	Will you belong to any organizations related to your occupational area or career?? List any leadership positions you have held.
Awards	example: School District Teacher of the Year, 2024

10 Year Resume Exercise

Name

Address

Phone Number

E-mail address

Educational Background

Employment History

Professional
Competencies

Professional Affiliations

Awards

Myth #14 - Once you earn your college degree, you'll be done with school for the rest of your life.

Students often look at college as something they must get through so they can compete for jobs. Many students look forward to the day they'll graduate and be done with college once and for all. In reality, you should plan to return to school periodically throughout your career. You may need to re-enroll in college to earn new certificates or credentials related to your occupation, or for ongoing professional training and development. This is true for teachers and dentists and people who work with computers, especially taking into consideration how quickly technology changes! Even if your job does not require you to take additional college courses, you may find that you want to do so to be promoted at work, or simply because you want to learn something new. Making a commitment now to life-long learning will enable you to take advantage of educational opportunities that come your way (such as your employer offering tuition subsidies if you go back to school). You may also find that after having been a college student for so many years, you'll actually miss being in a classroom setting after you graduate. You may even find that learning new material is actually fun. If you have difficulty finding a job in your career area when you graduate, consider enrolling at your local community college to enhance specific job skills (e.g., computer proficiency) or to add one or more job training certificates to your resume. The employee who is open to learning his or her entire career will most likely be considered over others with less education and training for promotions and new job assignments. When you cross the stage at your college graduation ceremony, be open to returning to school to keep your professional skills up-to-date, and to continue to be marketable as you move through the work force.

FAQ: Can I skip any math or English classes (i.e., take something other than what is recommended by my placement test scores)?

Many colleges and universities require new students to take an assessment or placement test in English and Math in order to determine the level where they should start in these subjects. Sometimes, Academic Counselors will also consult your high school transcripts to determine your placement in Math and English courses. If it has been awhile since you have been in school, you may not score as high on these assessments as you would have if you had taken them right after high school. You may want to spend some time reviewing the math you took in high school or recently prior to taking the assessment tests. It is advisable not to ignore suggested course placements based on your assessment scores. Professors rely on the accurate placement of students in the appropriate level courses (i.e., they want to make sure you can handle a certain level of work or have reviewed certain foundational concepts prior to taking their class). If you believe your assessment scores really do not reflect your academic ability, ask your Academic Counselor to take other factors (such as high school courses completed) into consideration when making course placements for you.

KEY CONCEPT: When it comes to mastering subject matter, there are no shortcuts.

Case Study: The English Requirements

Thao's family moved to the U.S when he was 15 years old. After high school he enrolled at the local community college. He was excited about his goal to transfer from the community college to a university as a Business major with an emphasis in Accounting Information Systems. He completed his English as a Second Language classes his first year at the community college. He began to take transfer-level courses, even though he was still working on mastering the English language. Thao became frustrated at what he considered the slow pace of his English classes. He could converse fluently in English with his friends, although he sometimes struggled to find the exact words to get his message across. When he met with an academic counselor, she urged him to focus on strengthening his English skills before venturing into more difficult classes that required extensive reading and written reports. She pointed out that he still had four sequential English courses he had to take before he could transfer to the university as a Business major. "It's important for you to become strong in the English language in order to be successful in your career," she said. "In addition, you will have to pass a writing proficiency test in order to graduate from the university. All students have to pass this test, no matter which major they choose." Thao was doing well in his math and computer classes; he felt frustrated that he was required to take so many English classes. He had attempted some General Education classes, but was disappointed with the low grades he'd earned. He felt like he understood the textbook language, but when it came to written tests and research papers, he'd receive low grades. Thao's friend told him about an English professor that never checked to see if his students had taken the English prerequisites to get into his class. "Why don't you just skip the prerequisites and register for Professor Dorsa's English Composition class? If you do, you'll be able to transfer to the university a whole year earlier! Everyone knows those assessment tests and all the classes they make you take are a waste of time anyway!" Thao thought about what his counselor had told him and then about what his friend had just suggested. When it came time to register for the next semester's classes, Thao scrolled through the online Class Schedule to the section listing the English classes being offered. At the top of the page he saw Professor Dorsa was schedule to teach three sections of the English Composition class. He sat down at his computer and logged on to the college's website, then clicked on the tab that read "Register For Classes."

1)   Should Thao follow his friend's advice? Why or why not?

2)   Does Thao really need to focus on his English writing skills if he is going to major in Accounting Information systems?

3) List the ways a Business Major would be required to be proficient in written and verbal communication.

4) How might Thao be required to be skilled in English as someone working in Accounting Information Systems?

5) Why do so many universities require their students to pass a Writing Proficiency Exam in order to graduate, when they most likely have already taken several Composition courses or classes that require extensive writing?

KEY CONCEPT: College is the time to develop transferable skills that will pay off throughout your career.

Senior Project

Some universities require students to complete a Senior Project in order to graduate. The Senior Project gives you the opportunity to take all that you have learned, and present something you have written or created that demonstrates that you have mastered the skills required in your major. Your Senior Project is a great opportunity to demonstrate the critical thinking skills you have developed in college, such as creative problem solving. Instead of producing something that has been done by many other students, think of a new approach and wow your professors. A great Senior Project is something that you can proudly elaborate on during job interviews. Employers will be interested in knowing that you were an active learner throughout college and will be able to contribute new ideas in the work environment.

Things You Should Find Out About Graduation:

- The number of units you need to graduate
- The number of General Education units you will need to graduate (and the areas of study)
- The minimum GPA you need to graduate
- Any competencies you must meet to graduate (e.g., math, writing)
- How many math courses you will need, and the required sequence
- How many writing courses you will need, and the required sequence
- Whether any of the courses you are taking do not count towards graduation requirements (e.g., prerequisites or foundational courses in writing, math, etc.)
- The deadline to file for graduation (usually a year before you actually graduate)

Other Things To Find Out:

- How to calculate your GPA (grade point average)
- What the requirements are to complete a minor in another area
- What graduate schools will want you to have taken prior to applying to their programs
- The process for clearing up any incomplete grades
- If your university career center offers workshops on resume writing and effective job interviewing
- Whether there is a faculty member in your department that advises students planning to go on to graduate school (e.g. required exams, assistance with personal statements, etc.)
- The cost of taking classes during summer session

How To Stay Motivated In College

Here are a few tips to help keep you going, when the going gets tough!

- Spend some time researching the benefits of completing your college degree.

- Review charts outlining your expected earnings over a lifetime based on the college degree(s) you plan to earn. Know the kind of lifestyle you want to have, and what it will take to get there.

- Remember that approximately 80% of all future jobs will require some type of postsecondary education.

- Know why you are in college. Some students enroll in college because they have to in order to enter a certain career. Some enroll because they feel it will buy them some time before entering the workforce, and they're not sure what they want to do career-wise. It's OK to admit "I'm not really sure why I'm here." Knowing your own motivation for being in college can help to keep you coming back each semester, quarter, or year.

- Actively seek out mentors who have already completed the degree you are earning, or who are working in the career area you plan to enter.

- Identify potential obstacles that could keep you from completing your college degree. Brainstorm possible solutions to overcome these obstacles.

- Ask your professors and advisors to share their own college experience with you. You'll find that many of your mentors may have struggled with some of their college courses or with deciding on a major.

- Make sure you have an up to date Educational Plan that outlines the courses you will need to complete to earn your degree. This should be broken down by semesters or quarters. Always have a Plan B in case you can't enroll in the courses you need when you need them.

- Meet with your Academic Counselor or Advisor at least once per year to make sure you stay on track academically. Seek out a professional mental health counselor if you are struggling with issues that are affecting your school work.

- Think about what you know you don't want to be or to happen in your life, and work backwards. What can you do to make sure those things don't occur? Set clear goals for your future.

- Have fun! Look for opportunities to make the learning environment more interesting. Interact with other students through class discussions and group projects, and build in opportunities to get to know your classmates outside of class.

Conclusion:

Rate yourself at the end of your first year of college (on a scale of 1 – 10, with 1 being the highest possible score). If you've been in college for a while, rate yourself on this past school year. How did you do in the following areas? What did you do well (that you should continue to do)? What do you want to change for next semester/year? What are some things you need to work on to achieve your academic and career goals? Don't forget to take what you've learned about being a successful student and share it with others who are new to the college environment!

____ Transitioning to college

____ Note-taking

____ Preparing for exams

____ Making good use of study time

____ Having clear goals

____ Choosing a major

____ Having an up to date Educational Plan

____ Meeting major/degree/graduation requirements

____ Managing finances

____ Time Management

____ Active Learning (e.g., actively participating in classes)

____ Participating in study groups

____ Working well in teams

____ Accessing campus resources

____ Visiting professors during their office hours

____ Developing a support network

____ Staying healthy in college

____ Meeting and interacting with people from diverse backgrounds

____ Getting involved in extracurricular activities (e.g., student clubs)

____ Developing Leadership Skills

____ Preparing for the world of work

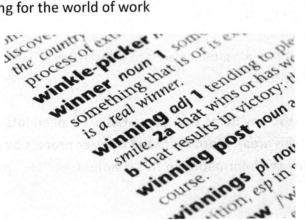

Self-Assessment

Rate yourself on the behaviors of successful students on a scale of 1 – 5. How well prepared are you in the following areas?

> 1 = I need lots of help with this
>
> 2 = I could do better in this area
>
> 3 = I'm OK in this area
>
> 4 = I do a good job in this area
>
> 5 = I'm very good at this

TRANSFER STUDENTS

____ I have stopped by my college's Transfer Center t learn more about the resources for transfer students.

____ I know the name of an Academic Counselor who can advise me about transferring to a university (if applicable) and how to select my classes so I can transfer

____ I know how much money I could save on earning my Bachelor's Degree by starting at a community college and transferring to a four year university

____ I know where to find articulation agreements between my community college and the universities to which I am interested in transferring

____ I am aware of guaranteed transfer admission agreements available to students enrolled at my community college

____ I know which courses in my transfer plan count for General Education, lower division major requirements, etc.

____ I keep a written list of questions related to transferring so I can ask these when I meet with Transfer Advisors.

Place a checkmark next to any items that you rated a 1 (I need lots of help with this) or a 2 (I could do better in this area). Learn more the transfer process by meeting with Transfer Advisors, and reviewing the information in this chapter (see "50 Tips For Transferring To A University").

Self Assessment

Rate yourself on the behaviors of successful students on a scale of 1 – 5. How well prepared are you in the following areas?

      1 = I need lots of help with this

      2 = I could do better in this area

      3 = I'm OK in this area

      4 = I do a good job in this area

      5 = I'm very good at this

CAREER SUCCESS

____   I know what employers are looking for in recent college graduates

____   I can articulate where I would like to be career-wise in 10 – 20 years

____   I own a nice suit or outfit I can wear to internship and job interviews

____   I have an up-to-date resume I can use to apply for jobs and internships

____   I participate in campus pre-professional organizations to learn more about my career area and to network with others in my field

____   I plan to complete an internship in my career area prior to graduating

____   I take advantage or resume writing and job interviewing workshops before I embark on a job search

____   I pay attention to and actively nurture my professional network

____   I have developed a 20 year "Career Ladder" outlining the steps I need to follow to achieve my career goals

Place a checkmark next to any items that you rated a 1 (I need lots of help with this) or a 2 (I could do better in this area). Meet with a Career Counselor at your college's Career Center and develop a "To Do" list to make sure you are well prepared to apply for internships, summer jobs, and permanent employment after graduation.

Chapter Notes:

Things to think about...

Things to remember...

Things to do....

End Notes

All articles adapted from the Cosumnes River College (Los Rios Community College District) New Student Guidebook, 2nd edition, 2008, were originally written and/or compiled/edited by Sharon Padilla-Alvarado.

The Case Studies were used in Cosumnes River College's Freshman Seminar and were originally written by Sharon Padilla-Alvarado.

Other books reviewed in writing How To Play & Win The College Game include:

Becoming A Master Student by Dave Ellis, 12th Edition, 2009; Focus On Community College Success, by Constance Staley, Annotated Instructor's Ed., 2000; On Course by Skip Downing, 4th Edition, 2005; Case Studies for the First Year (An Odyssey into Critical Thinking and Problem Solving) by Robert M. Sherfield, Rhonda J. Montgomery, & Patricia G. Moody, 2004; Foundations: A Reader For New College Students (California State University, Sacramento) by Virginia N. Gordon and Thomas L. Minnick, 4th Edition, 2007

The author has made every effort to ensure the accuracy of information presented in How to Play & Win The College Game, and to credit sources cited in researching the book. It is critical that students embarking on a college career work closely with Academic Advisors or Academic Counselors from their own college/university to ensure that they receive information on admissions requirements, majors, programs, transfer requirements, and graduation requirements specific to their own college or university. The author shall not be held liable for any damages arising from the book's content. This book is intended as a general guide for new college students (with an emphasis on first generation college students), and information specific to different colleges can, and will vary from campus to campus.

Chapter 1

"Getting Started: What Are Your Personal Goals?" adapted from New Student Guidebook, Cosumnes River College

Chapter 2

"Inappropriate Classroom Behavior" adapted from "Expectations For Classroom Behavior" New Student Guidebook, Cosumnes River College

Chapter 3

"Supplies Checklist" adapted from New Student Guidebook, Cosumnes River College

Chapter 4

"Time Management Prioritization Exercise" adapted from a Resident Advisor Training Worksheet, Housing Department, California Polytechnic State University, San Luis Obispo, 1983.

"Time Management And Schedule Building Tips" adapted from "Time Management Tips" New Student Guidebook, Cosumnes River College

Chapter 5

"What I Wish I'd Known In College" adapted from Cosumnes River College's Freshman Seminar curriculum (Sharon Padilla-Alvarado original author)

Chapter 6

"Money Management: Pat's Budget" and "John's Budget" adapted from Cosumnes River College's Freshman Seminar curriculum (Sharon Padilla-Alvarado original author)

Chapter 7

Learning Styles section based on information from LDPride.net http://www/ldpride.net/learningstyles.MI.htm

"How To Avoid Academic Probation" adapted from New Student Guidebook, Cosumnes River College

Reading reviewed for Note-taking Section includes "The Note-taking Process Flows" Becoming A Master Student by Dave Ellis, 12th Edition, 2009, and "Taking Lecture Notes: Different Strokes For Different Folks" by Constance Staley, Focus On Community College Success, Annotated Instructor's Edition, 2000.

Chapter 8

Information in the section on Academic Integrity based on material found on UCLA's website: http://www/library.ucla.edu/bruinsuccess

"Mid-Semester Questionnaire" developed for Cosumnes River College's Freshman Seminar (Sharon Padilla-Alvarado original author)

Chapter 9

Sources reviewed for section on Critical Thinking include: Learning To Think things Through (A Guide To Critical Thinking Across The Curriculum) by Gerald M. Nosich, 2011

Critical Thinking Across The Curriculum by Diane F. Halpern, 1997

"Critical Thinking Example" based on "Quick Flip Questions For Critical Thinking" by Linda G. Barton, based on the original Bloom's Taxonomy

"Problem Solving Exercise" adapted from The Interaction Method Problem Solving & Decision Making Model by Michael Doyle and Dave Strauss (from a training session, San Francisco, 1982)

"Almost 101 Ways To Earn Money For College" list compiled by Winters High School students in the U.C. Davis EdForward Program, January 2014

Chapter 11

Sources cited/reviewed in section on "Alcohol Awareness" include: http://www.fresnobee Becoming A Master Student, Chapter 11 - Health by Dave Ellis http://www.collegedrinkingprevention.gov "The Dark Power of Fraternities" by Caitlin Flanagan, The Atlantic, March 2014 http://mayoclinic.org/diseases/alcohol-poisoning/basic/symptoms http://www.collegedrinkingprevention.gov/OtherAlcoholInformation/factsAboutAlcohol http://awareawakealive.org/knowthesigns http://www/projectknow.com/research/alcohol_poisoning

Chapter 12

"What Employers Want In College Graduates" and "The Secretary's Commission On Achieving Necessary Skills (SCANS)" Adapted from the U.S. Department of Labor, What Work Requires Of Schools – A SCANS Report For America